PERSONAL TUTORING

IN ACTION

A HANDBOOK FOR STAFF INVOLVED IN WORKING WITH AND SUPPORTING STUDENTS

By Colin Lago and Geraldine Shipton

Sheffield University Counselling Service

2nd Edition Revised and Updated by
Colin Lago and Safina La Peta Meah

This booklet is available for (bulk and single) purchase by colleges and universities. For further details, please contact:

The Secretary
University Counselling Service
Mushroom Lane, Sheffield S10 2TS
United Kingdom

DISCLAIMER

We are most grateful to colleagues who have granted us permission to reproduce their material in this booklet. In certain instances, despite our attempts to locate copyright permission, we have been unable to do so and should there be a further edition of this publication we will be delighted to make full and appropriate acknowledgements of these instances.

Personal Tutoring in Action by Colin Lago and Geraldine Shipton

First Published in Great Britain in 1994
by the Sheffield University Counselling Service

Copyright © 1994 Colin Lago and Geraldine Shipton

Printed by the Printing Resources Centre, Sheffield University.

2nd edition revised and updated by Colin Lago and Safina Meah 1999.

Sheffield University Counselling Service
Mushroom Lane, Sheffield S10 2TS
United Kingdom

CONTENTS

1. FOREWORD

I am delighted to provide a Foreword to this second edition of the Personal Tutoring in Action Handbook. I am sure that it will prove to be a valuable guide to new tutors and a reminder to more experienced tutors. It provides a wealth of ideas, information and support to assist in the complex and challenging role of personal tutoring.

As the University of Sheffield plays its part in achieving greater student numbers and widening access to higher education, we all need to think carefully about how to make best use of our time. Effective tutoring has a vital role to play in the learning process today. Facilitating the personal development of students is a significant element of the higher education process, and one to which we must take a proactive approach.

Complementary to the University's commitment to our students' welfare is a willingness to help staff acquire skills and develop expertise through courses and resource materials such as this handbook.

Professor Sir Gareth Roberts
Vice Chancellor
The University of Sheffield

2. THE ROLE OF THE PERSONAL TUTOR

Personal tutoring has long been recognised as a cornerstone of British higher education. The tutoring relationship is only one of an historically long line of such relationships in which the development of the learner is fostered in the tutelage of the 'wise elder'. Despite this noble and long history, staff are seldom trained in the skills of student support, and increasingly with new demands and larger student populations, staff contact with students is likely to decrease.

This booklet has thus been written to assist staff in this aspect of their work.

The role of the tutor is a complex one. There are many 'models' used by departments that range from explicit, constructed systems where the role of tutoring is embedded in the working practices of the department, to other informal models of departments who have personal tutors, but lack systems for establishing regular contact with students. Other approaches include that of 'social tutors' where the onus is on the tutor to establish a small social grouping of students that have the opportunity of meeting, from time to time, for tutorial purposes.

Interestingly, in a booklet on Tutoring written by Miller in 1983, no definition of tutoring is offered. Rather, the writer offers a constellation model depicting a variety of skills that tutors may require, from time to time, as circumstances demand.

The underlying intentions of tutoring are geared towards enabling students to achieve, to learn successfully, (both academically as well as developmentally) to be able to become responsible for themselves and to be discerning in their processes of judgement. Many more aims could easily be added to this list. However, just from the brief list of intentions above it can be seen that the skills required of tutorial staff span a range from teaching to 'mentoring', from pastoral interventions to disciplinary confrontations. Such a list of qualities and skills is daunting. Miller points out, however, the value of team work: "...it is not expected that each tutor will take on such a range of tasks for each student. The intention is rather that each task is available for each student. This means that a particularly important task for course teams is to determine who does what and by when."

The overall aims of this booklet are to offer individual staff, tutors (and others who are in supportive contact with students) some theoretical insights into the importance of communication processes, for these underlie all interactions between staff and students and ideas on how these skills may be acquired. Also included are sections detailing the needs of particular groups of students, personal accounts of tutoring by experienced staff in the University and some ideas related to working with groups and fostering good study skills practice.

A sample job description for a tutor (from Miller 1983) is included in Appendix II. The important point made, however, is that departmental teams devise explicit strategies for managing the tutorial aspect of their educational work, thus ensuring that all students in their department may benefit from this provision. This will shift the task of tutoring from an accidental, incidental and ad hoc process to one that is embodied in the structure and aims of the department's work.

We are also cognisant of the substantial range of student support work engaged in by clerical, technical and administrative staff. Consequently, though we most often refer to tutors in the text, this booklet is written to inform and support all staff working with students. In our turn, we hope that we may be supportive of all those engaged in fostering student development and trust that this booklet will contribute to the general thrust of this work.

Colin Lago and Geraldine Shipton
University Counselling Service 1993

Addendum to the Role of the Personal Tutor (for this 2nd edition)

ADDENDUM

Since the first publication of this booklet in 1993 substantial developments have occurred in the further and higher education sectors. Quality assessments proce- dures of both teaching and research activity have been introduced and the impact of scores gained by departments in these exercises may well be extremely instrumental in the future in relation to research funding and focus of academic work.

An element entitled Student Support and Guidance is strongly featured in teaching and research assessment procedures and academic departments, alongside student welfare services are required to give evidence of the various means by which students are supported through their studies.

A new policy has also been adopted within Sheffield University that decrees that all undergraduate students have a named personal tutor. Similar developments have occurred elsewhere.

The introduction of a student charter, determined originally by national initiatives and developed locally within many universities means that a range of rights and responsibilities have now been laid out as templates of good educational practice towards students.

The continued expansion of higher education, paralleled by dramatic changes to student funding have also had a dramatic effect on both student and staff experiences of higher education.

In short, the above changes, still in process, are likely to increase pressures on universities and colleges to ensure that sensitive, coherent and practical procedures are firmly in place to facilitate the overall personal and academic development of students. It is hoped that this book will continue to prove useful to support staff.

Several new sections have been added since the first edition. These include:

a) ideas derived from Barbara Rickinson's work on student retention at the University of Birmingham.

b) helpful suggestions in relation to bereavement, student illness, (physical and psychological).

c) dealing with difficult and disruptive students.

d) harassment issues.

Following our experience of the first edition, where interest was also shown in this booklet by colleagues in other British and overseas Universities, we have attempted to keep to an appropriate (yet necessary) minimum number of references to services internal to the University of Sheffield. For those readers outside the University, we ask you to understand our need to include the internal references as this booklet was primarily written for internal purposes.

Colleagues in other universities have generously given permission for the reproduction of their original materials and these include:

Dr Barbara Rickinson (University of Birmingham)

Anne Heyno (University of Westminster)

Eunice Mathers (Humberside University)

Patsy Taylor (University of Liverpool)

My gratitude is extended to Christine Davison who has tirelessly typed the script and Safina La Peta Meah who assisted in preparing new documents for this second edition.

Colin Lago
Autumn 1999

3. PRIMARY AIMS FOR PERSONAL TUTORING

- To facilitate personal development of tutees

- To monitor progress of tutees

- To provide link between students and University authorities

- To be a responsible adult within the organisation in whom the student can confide.

- To intervene with the University authorities on behalf of their tutees.

From *A Handbook for Personal Tutors*
by Sue Wheeler and Jan Birtle
Open University Press 1993

4. TUTORING AND COUNSELLING IN HIGHER EDUCATION

I have now spent around twenty years as a University Tutor (a Pathologist), and in that time I have seen many students (and staff) with major or minor problems which have needed attention. If I were asked, however, "where does lecturing/tutoring end and counselling start?" I would have to say "I don't know" - these activities overlap considerably. Students arrive on my courses with their own cocktail of personality types, attitudes to work and problems, into which are shaken (not stirred) home sickness, and stresses of personal and academic life. In my 'lecturer' role I have to design courses, teaching sessions and assessments with this potentially dangerous cocktail in mind. A university course should be challenging, but some areas in my course are more likely to be difficult for students than others, and I must be alert whilst teaching to detect abnormal reactions to these at an early stage, when developing problems are addressed most easily. Most students (and staff) do not recognise or acknowledge problems, or initiate problem-solving actions, until they are already in great difficulty. I have found that unplanned 'out of teaching' contacts (e.g. in corridors) with individual students who seem to have problems can be very valuable; 'early' gentle conversational interventions such as "you look a little tired/sad/worried today - how are things?" can provide a usually welcomed opportunity for the student to voice problems, many of which are minor, and can be addressed and solved before they spiral towards disaster. This tutoring/counselling process helps the student to learn more about themselves, their feelings, and their personal interaction with the world. I believe that this is just as important a part of their university learning as the subject matter of their course, but unfortunately this is the most neglected area of university learning.

Most problems that students have are minor, and can be addressed with sympathy, care and a 'problem-solving' approach which encourages the student to explore areas of personal difficulty and to develop coping strategies in a supporting (but preferably not "leading") environment. However, sudden and major problems can occur at times; examples are bereavement, illness or serious psychiatric problems such as anxiety, depression, attempted suicide or psychotic disorders such as schizophrenia. These can be time-consuming, and extremely difficult and upsetting for tutors to address personally, particularly when we are under considerable pressure of work or have our own problems. Knowing our own limitations and 'when to refer' a student to the University Counselling Service or the Student Health Service is important - these Services protect and support university members confronted with situations which are beyond our skills, and their advice is freely available and confidential.

I believe that 'counselling' is an essential component of good teaching and tutoring in a caring university such as ours. Universities have to acknowledge that, with increasing pressures on academics to 'produce results' in research, there is a danger that, in the academic bustle, our humanity is squeezed out. Like all of us, students (and colleagues who also have their share of personal problems) need to feel loved and supported. Providing this support is highly rewarding to tutors, but it also provides a caring role model for students, and a vital component of their continuing education. At a rather philosophical level, tutors each have a small but important part to play in exerting a positive influence on the future of humanity.

Dr Andy Parsons,
Senior Lecturer in Ophthalmic Pathology,
Director, Ophthalmic Sciences Unit

5. TRANSITIONS

"Change of any kind is one of the monumental stress factors of our time".

Lyn Eaker

"Transition is a period of moving from one state of certainty to another, with an interval of uncertainty and change in between."

Naomi Golan
(1981)

This involves an ending, a loss and an anxious stage of doubt and confusion when old rules no longer prevail and previous ways of behaving seem to be less adequate before it becomes clear that new possibilities are on the horizon.

Students, as a body, are a population in transition. They come into higher education for a limited amount of time. They come from somewhere else and after 2, 3 or 4 years will move on to something else.

Processes of transition are both exciting and stressful. One aspect of transition, that of homesickness, is an underestimated area that can cause considerable levels of personal discomfort to students in the first few months (if not longer) of their courses.

HOME STUDENTS: HOMESICKNESS

"Thank you for making this topic respectable. For years I grieved at University, I was so unhappy, no-one ever knew. I was ashamed to say. It was my private hell. I couldn't bring myself to enjoy anything. No one ever knew. I even contemplated suicide".

(Female graduate recalling student days by letter to Shirley Fisher 1989)

A major body of research on the topic of homesickness was carried out by Dr Shirley Fisher in recent years. The widespread and debilitating effects of this transition process are demonstrated by the following quotes.

"However defined, about 60 per cent of samples of students report having the experience of homesickness.

...There are no sex or age differences in those reporting homesickness. About 5 to 10 per cent report the experience as prolonged and distressing... Studies carried out at the University of Manchester have recently shown that there is an association with lowered health... lowered concentration and raised inefficiency ...in those who are homesick... It can be present in populations of second, third and fourth year students, although the incidence declines to about 30 or 40 per cent.

The study revealed another interesting result: all student groups whether homesick or not showed a rise in depression and absent-mindedness following the move to residence in University. This suggests that the transition to University is a stressful event for all who undertake it. Analysis of self-reported stressful problems by students in the first term indicated that academic concerns were paramount...

Second on the list of frequently reported problems were financial worries. Thirty six per cent of students reported being worried by the need to make grants last and there was a fear of not being able to buy necessary books in order to keep up with academic requirements. There was also guilt expressed concerning ultimate dependence on parental support".

Because there is great psychological disturbance and absentmindedness there may be inefficiency and loss of concentration which compounds the problem because early failure and difficulty may have knock-on effects. Analysis of self-reported problems by students confirms this even fuller. Reports by students show that over 70% fear the new academic demands, feel threatened by lectures, the standards required, the lack of clear boundaries for success. They feel overwhelmed and lost, experience constant concern about studying and coping and fear letting parents down. Further on in her publication Fisher says "An unexpected result of a recent pilot study is that by Spring and Summer terms psycho-neurotic symptoms are still elevated relative to base levels prior to leaving home. Depression, anxiety, absent-mindedness and somatic symptoms are the main symptoms raised".

Please note that these studies were carried out on British students attending institutions of higher education in Britain. Homesickness, given the above incidence of its effects, whilst often unpleasant and indeed sometimes debilitating, can also be seen to be a normal human response to the changes incurred. Students can often be reassured on this aspect if they know that what they are experiencing is an inevitable response to transition. Despite its 'normality' as a human reponse to transition it is most important that tutors also recognise and respect the emotional effects of this process on individuals.

Orientation and induction programmes have their part to play in easing this transition process for the student, offering opportunities for the establishment of social and working relationships in this new setting.

"The worst feeling in the world, lonely, frightened and missing home so badly - I missed the place, friends, food, the comfort of my bedroom. Phoning home made it worse. Letters from home caused near breakdown. I felt worse at night and first thing in the morning. Yet I never told anyone. I told my parents what fun it is at University."

(Male student, 22, reflecting on first term experience in Shirley Fisher's research).

INTERNATIONAL STUDENTS: CULTURE SHOCK

"Culture shock is a state of mind in transition, a state in which an individual's senses adapt to new stimuli and he becomes aware that his behaviour, which for years he had thought of as correct, polite and friendly, can be interpreted or misinterpreted as odd, rude and even hostile. It is a period in which his experience of life does not relate to life around him.

Culture shock, like love, is a temporary madness.

The most wonderful and most depressing feeling in the world. An experience to make life more complete".

(From: *Culture Shock Thailand and How to Survive It.*
Robert and Nanthapa Cooper.)

International students are a very specific group of students who experience difficulties of transition and homesickness. Sometimes known as "uprooting" or more popularly "culture shock", the process of settling down in a new country, a new culture, with a new place to live, new friends to make and new forms of study can present quite different barriers to overcome.

Research on culture shock indicates that there can be four or five different stages of the process. The following diagram demonstrates the wide ranging effects of settling down in a new culture.

The research also indicates that there is little predictability as to how long these effects last or indeed that each stage can be worked through satisfactorily to a comfortable sense of existence in the home country and the newly adopted one.

Given the psychological, affective and behavioural consequences arising from culture shock, it is indeed remarkable that the drop-out and failure rates for international students are not much higher.

A MODEL OF CULTURE SHOCK

Stages	Emotional Range	Effects on the Individual
Contact	excitement stimulation euphoria playfulness discovery	The individual is insulated by his or her own culture. Differences as well as similarities provide rationalisation for continuing confirmation of status, role and identity.
Disintegration	confusion disorientation loss apathy isolation loneliness inadequacy	Cultural differences begin to intrude. Growing awareness of being different leads to loss of self-esteem. Individual experiences loss of cultural support ties and misreads new cultural cues.
Reintegration	anger rage nervousness anxiety frustration	Rejection of second culture causes preoccupation with likes and dislikes, differences are projected. Negative behaviour,however is a form of self-assertion and growing self-esteem.
Autonomy	self-assured relaxed warm empathic	The individual is socially and linguistically capable of negotiating most new and different situations; he or she is assured of ability to survive new experiences.
Independence	trust humour love full range of previous emotions	Social, psychological, and cultural differences are accepted and enjoyed. The individual is capable of exercising choice, and responsibility and able to create meaning for situations.

From *The Transitional Experiences: Alternative View of Culture Shock*
By Adler, P.S.
Journal of Humanistic Psychology. 1975

6. HELPING STUDENTS SETTLE IN

Induction and Orientation

GENERAL INTRODUCTION

Research by Professor John Gardner into the effectiveness of induction and orientation courses in American Universities has revealed marked improvement in completion rates of degrees as a result of participation in their "Freshman Seminars". Similar experiences have also been reported by some British institutions of higher education.

As the nature of higher education becomes increasingly complex (credit accumulation, cross-discipline courses, distance learning modules etc.) and the range of students becomes wider a greater need exists to assist students in their successful entry into the process of higher education.

Many traditional induction/orientation events and courses within departments have comprised one or a series of mini-lectures, involving perhaps introductions to staff and an outline of the course. These components are, of course, very important. Other aspects that also require attention however include:

(a) the process of helping students feel more at home in their new situation.

(b) the stimulation of a group work ethos that underlies the importance of co-operation, mutual support and co-tutoring amongst students themselves and

(c) geographical orientation in relation to departments and facilities on the University campus and key features of the city.

Some tutorial staff have commented that with the onset, in recent years, of larger classes they have become aware of factors such as less social contact within the group, more students who appear isolated, sometimes higher failure and drop-out rates or increased incidence of transfer to other courses etc.

Induction programmes for courses must not only concentrate on an introduction to the course, the University and the staff (as is often the case) but must also enable staff/student and student/student introductions at a personal level to be effected, This is not necessarily an easy thing to achieve, but where it can occur successfully, students can begin to establish a social network. In the absence of explicit and structured systems for introductions, some students who lack confidence or are quieter in disposition may remain isolated.

In these circumstances, feelings of isolation combine with a sense of disorientation and pangs of homesickness may render the student less able to function socially or academically for what might be quite some time.

Induction can mean to bring artificially into life. The following four stage model for induction programmes might help when considering the construction of such courses.

1. **Pre-arrival induction** - typified by letters of welcome, open days, extended interview sessions, information interviews .... All these early contacts with students provide opportunities for beginning to create a climate of welcome and information.

2. **Day of arrival** - this can be a lonely day if all students have to do is register and locate their accommodation. If the day of arrival is a Friday, they can then experience a lonely weekend. Possibilities of contact with other contemporaries might be useful. Both academic departments and halls of residence can play a role in this regard. Students who are outside the traditional halls accommodation may have specific difficulties in this regard.

3. **Overall introduction: course and facilities** - organisation of induction programmes need to include a consideration of staff and room timetabling, appropriate introductions of staff and subjects, recognition of the role of allied support services (library, student services, physical education) and provide opportunities for informal meetings and communication between staff and students. Appropriate explanation of the purposes of lectures, tutorials, seminars, group work projects and other learning opportunities can be helpful at this early stage. Many students may not have a clear understanding of the aims, purposes and the behaviour required of them in the different educational activities in which they will be engaging. Such processes may best be discussed in smaller tutor groups rather than large lectures.

4. **Ongoing Induction** - induction can occur not only at the beginning of courses but at various points throughout the course when new phases of new subjects are introduced. By preparing the ground, so to speak, students are enabled to understand the overall context and interconnectedness of one unit with others. The specific academic expectations for this unit can also be spelt out, giving students the opportunity to prepare their work appropriately.

SOME STRUCTURED FORMS OF INTRODUCTIONS

A variety of mechanisms exist for enabling (a) staff and students and (b) students and students to meet and introduce themselves. The underlying purpose for such activity is to provide a structured opportunity, within the course programme, for students to have the opportunity for establishing primary social contact as this will relieve an immediate sense of social isolation. If such personal concerns are reduced, opportunities for learning are maximised.

Here is one example:

1. Get students to introduce themselves to another student in the class (perhaps their neighbour) for between 2 and 5 minutes each way.

2. Then get those pairs of students to meet another pair. In this grouping of 4, the members of the original 2 pairs introduce their partner to the other 2.

3. The groups of 4 might then be invited to get into groups of 8 and perhaps just share names and place of origin.

4. These groupings then might be given a short task/or discussion theme that is course related, to discuss.

The above session could comfortably be fitted into a time slot lasting between 20 minutes and an hour. We would recommend that if staff choose to try this, it is important to (a) consider the location, (a raked lecture theatre does not allow mobility) (b) the ease with which furniture might be moved and (c) that it is introduced with sensitivity, noting any students who find the process difficult and making sure any single left over student is attached to a couple as soon as possible. There are many other ideas which could be incorporated into longer workshop programmes based upon an experiential approach to learning.

SOCIAL AND SPORTING EVENTS

The following ideas for integrating students into University departments have been incorporated by different faculties and schools over the years:

- Wine and cheese functions

- Parties/discos/dances

- Games/'Tiddlywinks'/Quizzes etc.

- Treasure hunt around the University - this enables an exploration of roads, departments, buildings.

- Staff vs. students sessions in a variety of activities available within or outside the University.

- Informal gatherings in the local public house
  Please note that this can sometimes make things difficult for certain students to join in because of their own backgrounds, cultures or beliefs.

Any of the above activities may be organised within the working days time-table or offered as an evening activity. In such cases it might be useful to consult the Students' Union Fresher's diary, thus trying to avoid clashes of dates with their own orientation programme.

The above events need not simply be idle bits of fun. They have the potential for enabling a variety of patterns of communication to occur between staff and students - a basis upon which more positive tutorial relationships can develop.

PEER SUPPORT/'BUDDY' SYSTEMS

Some Universities in this country and the USA have formally incorporated into their departmental processes systems for mutual support between students. Arrangements such as the following have been used:

1. links between freshers and 2nd or 3rd year students

2. occasional activities attracting cross year participation.

3. Volunteer 2nd or 3rd year students acting as mentor/guide to a small group of freshers.

4. Students being helped to form their own small 'reference' groups who agree to meet from time to time to share progress and support.

7. SYSTEMATIC MONITORING OF THE ADJUSTMENT TO UNIVERSITY OF UNDERGRADUATES

INTRODUCTION

"Students who were integrated in to the academic and social life of the institution were less likely to drop out" .

(Tinto 1975)

A recent figure recording the incidence of student withdrawal from universities suggests that approximately 17% of the student population withdrew from their courses during the academic year. (1994 -1995)

Inevitably, a huge variety of reasons will exist behind student decisions to withdraw, temporarily or permanently, from higher education. Culture shock, homesickness, wrong course choice, disappointment with course content, poor accommodation, inadequate finance, all feature highly in student responses. In many cases students would have been making very wise and appropriate decisions based on their initial experience at university. However, there will have been many more, who with sufficient support and monitoring would have continued towards academic success.

Student withdrawals, especially if inappropriate, are costly at both the human and economic levels. This paper reports recent research and offers a model of monitoring students progress, through tutoring during the first term.

RESEARCH FINDINGS

Recent research by Barbara Rickinson (1995) at the University of Birmingham revealed that "the degree to which students felt prepared, both academically and emotionally, for the transition to university, and the availability of appropriate academic and personal support at the transition stage were the two factors shown to affect student ability to make a commitment to university and their particular programme of study".

The above publication by Rickinson reported results gleaned from first year students at Birmingham University in their first term.

In a second research paper Rickinson (1996) has presented research findings based on postal questionnaires and follow up telephone interviews with all first year undergraduates (1993/94) who had withdrawn from Birmingham in their first, second and third terms. Course difficulties and living away from home were endorsed by the highest percentage of students in both groups.

In both study groups a high percentage of students sought help from their personal tutor.

The findings reported in the second study have continued to support the hypothesis that the major factor affecting withdrawal/persistence behaviour is the degree to which students can adjust to the new academic and social demands of the university environment. The ability to change and adjust to new situations varies from individual to individual. It requires the capacity to contain anxiety well enough to tolerate new learning. This capacity is influenced by a complex interplay of factors as indicated in the volume of research to date. However it needs to be remembered that entry to university also provides students with an important developmental opportunity to improve their adaptability. Attention needs to be focused on ways in which we can support students to use this opportunity. Systematic monitoring of first year undergraduates' adjustment to university at four/six weeks could be a strategy to ensure that students experiencing difficulties are given the opportunity to improve their ability to adjust.

STRATEGY FOR MONITORING THE ADJUSTMENT TO UNIVERSITY OF FIRST YEAR UNDERGRADUATES

The following adjustment monitoring system needs to be built into the existing departmental structures to avoid extra paperwork and to provide feedback that will be of value to the department. It is of central importance that confidentiality boundaries need to be respected when making records on students' files.

GUIDELINES FOR CONDUCTING TUTORIAL INTERVIEWS

Individual interview within first 4 - 6 weeks of first semester

This procedure should be the second stage, following initial induction and introductory interviews. (Ideas for induction and orientation programmes are featured in previous sections of this book).

Aims

1. To build a relationship which assists the monitoring of progress process.

2. To assess students' initial adjustment and motivation level.

3. To identify any difficulties, or requirements for extra academic or personal support.

4. To ensure that students are aware of the support available to them.

5. To identify students at risk of withdrawing.

6. To provide early warning of potential problems in course structure.

Interview Structure

1. Emphasise the collaborative nature of the interview and stress that it will in no way affect their academic marks.

2. Explain the focus of interview, time allocated and confidentiality boundaries.

3. Explore with open questions, all areas on the check list.

4. Summarise any difficulties and check with student for accuracy of understanding.

5. Based on the above information, circle a score for academic and social/personal adjustment on the attached form (to be kept on file).

6. Outline support available if appropriate. Ensure that you are aware of the range available.

ADJUSTMENT CHECK LISTS

These check lists should be used in an interview, assessing adjustment to university for first year undergraduates. Explore each category on the lists below then briefly summarise your overall impression of student adjustment for each of these categories. Based on this information, score the scale below each list.

Programme of study Checklist

● Initial experience of module content.

● Reason for choice of programme.

● Level of competence and prior academic experience.

● Management of course demands and workload.

● Requirement for extra academic support
(e.g. disability, language, study skills).

Satisfactory → At risk of withdrawing

1   2   3   4   5

Transition Checklist

● Initial experience of university life.

● Living away from home/in a different culture.

● Accommodation.

● Making friends, social activity.

● Interests.

● Balancing being a student with other responsibilities.

● Requirement for extra personal support
(e.g. personal difficulties requiring counselling / welfare advice).

Satisfactory → At risk of withdrawing

1   2   3   4   5

RECOMMENDED ACTION

A score of 2-3 for a given assessment list indicates a personal tutor may/should arrange a follow up interview. If these difficulties are not resolved, the senior tutor or year tutor should be consulted.

A score of 4-5 indicates the student may be referred to the senior tutor or year tutor urgently. The senior tutor may also liaise with, or refer to, the University counselling service.

Rickinson reports that "a pilot study of the system, in four schools/departments preparing for a visit from the Higher Education Funding Council Teaching Quality Assessment Team, provided the following feedback:

1. Systematic monitoring process also highlighted some potential difficulties in course structures. This information was of value to the department.

2. For students who withdrew, there was information to feed back into the admissions process.

3. The pilot study played a useful part in the preparation process for the Teaching Quality Assessment exercise, and provided valuable information to present to the assessors."

   "Every student withdrawal represents a lost opportunity for the individual student and a financial loss to the Institution... early identification of students at risk of withdrawing is essential"

The University Counselling Service can assist academic departments in the consideration of personal tutoring activity through attendance at departmental staff meetings, staff training workshops, liaison with and referral of students experiencing difficulties.

The authors wish to express their gratitude to Dr Barbara Rickinson at the University of Birmingham for granting permission to reproduce the above extracts from her research publications.

8. HELPING RELATIONSHIPS

There are multifarious ways of helping people with problems: giving practical help, advice or information; teaching; befriending; changing a structure or system within which the other person's difficulty is enmeshed; adopting an advocacy role; or at times, choosing to take an informal counselling approach. A personal tutor will find him or herself under pressure from a student or colleague or, indeed, from within their own self-expectations to fulfil many of these roles. This seems at first glance to be right and proper. However, all of these ways of helping have drawbacks as well as advantages in different situations and for different people.

HIDDEN FACTORS WHICH CAN INFLUENCE RELATIONSHIPS

It is not always clear which is the best strategy to adopt nor which is the most realistic (and the two things are sometimes different). Furthermore, the personal tutor will possibly be only dimly aware of his or her own unconscious responses to the person seeking help and probably, at first meeting, totally unaware of the unconscious or only half-glimpsed preconceptions the student has about the tutor. Such feelings may never be acknowledged by either party but they will certainly load the student-tutor relationship with hidden agendas, hopes and fears.

This 'hidden baggage' may be quite positive in some ways, for example, earlier experiences with teachers may have led the student to expect fair and encouraging treatment in a relationship based on trust and benign detachment. Unfortunately, some students will expect and even elicit misunderstanding or hostility. Quite appropriate and well-meant attempts to establish an opportunity to get to know a student in the cosy privacy of one's own office can feel dangerous to someone whose trust has been abused in the past and who may even have been sexually exploited in a previous situation. The range of possible variations in emotional 'flavour' of previous relationships to someone in authority are great. This means that you are liable to be experienced at times as much *less* or much *more* wise/caring/overworked/powerful/knowledgeable than you really are!

The answer to being able to deal with this quite normal transference of earlier feelings about other people onto the current relationship in question is not necessarily to rapidly enrol on the next mind-reading course but to keep an open mind about how the student is seeing you and to systematically seek feedback about what you think you have agreed to do with the student. One student may find your willingness to do all you can to help with his or her problems the ideal match for his or her reluctance to take control of their own life while another student may interpret the same eagerness as prying and patronising.

Similarly, it may be equally important to clarify what you are not going to be doing. For example, a student may be considering changing to a different course. You may want to help the student take a well-informed view of the choices that are available as well as estimating the likelihood of the department concerned being amenable to taking on a transferred student. It will have been useful to explore the reasons for a change. You may wish to refer the person to the Students' Union Advice Centre if there are financial or other considerations to take into account. However, all of these factors and probably a lot more have to be weighed up by the student. It is natural to try and get someone else to make a decision for you when consequences are hard to evaluate but it is in a situation just like this that the tutor needs to stand back and check out what is going on and who it is that is taking responsibility. Be explicit and get the student to recap the discussion, the steps he or she has to take next, what it is you will or won't be doing and finally decline invitations to make the decision yourself. If it doesn't work out for the student you could be blamed but more importantly, it really is the student's responsibility.

The psychological history we all bring to relationships is further complicated by cultural, racial and sexual differences of which we may not be aware. We will look more closely at some of this later but no handbook can prepare us for the enormous diversity of people with whom we meet in a University. We can however remain open to the idea that our own way of viewing any interaction is only one of many interpretations.

WHAT ARE THE BOUNDARIES WHICH DEFINE THE WAY I OPERATE AS A PERSONAL TUTOR?

The process of delineating responsibilities within a personal tutorial in the way described are part and parcel of establishing boundaries about your role as a personal tutor. Some boundaries can be set up in advance of meetings. You may wish to be available 'on tap' to your students by creating a routine where students can drop in at any time to see you. Or you will have decided that students must book to see you in some way or that your 'drop in' period is open only at specified times. Whatever is your preferred style, make it clear and public.

In much the same fashion you will need to tell students how much time they can spend with you and make arrangements for times which are convenient to you as well as the student. Students do tend to believe that lectures are prepared and delivered effortlessly and generally know little about 'admin' demands on your time.

Research is sometimes thought of almost as if it is the preferred activity relegating the student to second place.

You will need to be able to find a location which is sufficiently private if you choose to take a counselling approach or much less private if you want to discourage this way of being related to at certain times or with certain people. Tutors who have no access to a private office may choose to stroll somewhere quiet in order to chat without being disturbed. Make sure the student understands why you are taking this measure and is amenable to such a strategy.

These boundaries around time, place and 'contract' about what is being done are in some ways the simpler aspects of boundary making. Other more sensitive areas include making decisions about how far friendliness extends into friendship. You may feel quite relaxed with the idea of socialising with groups of tutees or individual students. You may be able to wear different 'hats' on different occasions and move happily from being a supportive listener to dealing with disciplinary matters. Not everyone finds the conflict of roles easy to negotiate but everyone does have to be aware of responsibilities both to the individual student and the department. You may see your own impartiality in a better light than others do. Remember you have to be seen to be fair as well as to be fair.

CONFIDENTIALITY

The other great boundary dilemma is about confidentiality. Keeping absolute confidentiality is extremely difficult and outside of the confessional is rare. Professional counsellors are obliged under law to divulge information in some circumstances but otherwise try to erect strong defences around private information (including the simple facts about whether or not a student has attended for counselling). Personal tutors will be expected to pass on some information about their students within the department. Students need to know where they stand in this respect and it is much easier to manage delicate situations where trust can easily be betrayed if you can give the students a clear idea about your true position.

This is beneficial in several ways: some students firmly believe that everything that is noticed in a perjorative way about themselves is recorded and stored away to be used in evidence against them and are surprised and relieved that this is not the case.

As a society we are beginning to be more careful about the implications of keeping information about people on paper or in computers. However, we tend to be far more casual about verbal exchanges and are easily lured into gossiping. It is really hard to deflect inappropriate questions from curious colleagues but it may be a useful skill to acquire!

9. HELPFUL SKILLS AND QUALITIES IN COMMUNICATION

INTRODUCTION

The following modes of communication will hopefully enhance your effectiveness in responding to students needs and problems. However simple some of the following suggestions may appear, their consistent practice frequently falls down.

An important component in the tutoring process is that of the RELATIONSHIP between tutor and tutee. There may be many instances where a student, seeking help from a tutor, does not have a previous relationship with them. In other circumstances, the tutor may know the student well from previous teaching and tutorial contact.

Whatever the circumstances, it can be helpful to conceive of the tutoring process as one which takes place within the context of RELATEDNESS between the tutor and tutee. Tutoring is not a mechanistic process and indeed with the present trend for larger classes, greater use of technology and distance learning, the act of tutoring may become the human interface of the educational process.

The following skills, therefore, are recommended as vital components within the tutoring relationship. Extensive research has been carried out on the application of some of the following skills within the tutoring domain and their effects upon educational development are considerable. More information upon this aspect is provided in Appendix 1.

HELPFUL SKILLS

"Do not judge another until you have walked for two moons
in their moccasins"

A Native American Indian Saying

ACCEPTANCE

The quality of acceptance of the individual, whatever they look like, whoever they are, in a manner that is non-judgemental, is crucial as a basis for the formation fo a helping/learning relationship. Beyond feeling acceptance, however, it is important if the tutor can demonstrate or communicate that acceptance to the tutee.

At first glance, this quality seems simple enough. However, research from social psychology indicates that human beings have a tendency to be judging others within a minute of meeting them. Our judgements about others, of course, say a lot about ourselves, our own backgrounds, our attitudes, prejudices and so on. The way people dress, cut their hair, talk, and behave are all focii for our judgemental tendencies.

A useful exercise in personal awareness, here, is to imagine for a few moments what would be your 'nightmare tutee'. Someone whom you would be very hard pressed to feel any acceptance of whatsoever. What would they look like, how would they behave? What would they be setting off in you? Also, if such a person actually approached you for assistance, how might you handle this situation?

Unaccepting responses to others would include not inviting the person in to the office, not inviting them to sit down, not establishing eye contact, continuing one's own work etc. Once into conversation such responses would comprise elements such as generalising, avoiding the tutee's meanings, being cynical, impatient or judgemental in response.

Research indicates that it is not only useful to feel acceptance of the other but to be able to demonstrate that facility. In communicating non-critical acceptance one is conveying a respect for the 'worthwhileness' of the other person.

LISTENING

Listening attentively to others with all the components described below in the Chinese word is a very challenging activity indeed. Our attention wanders, we might be pre-occupied with what we were doing before this person arrived and so on.

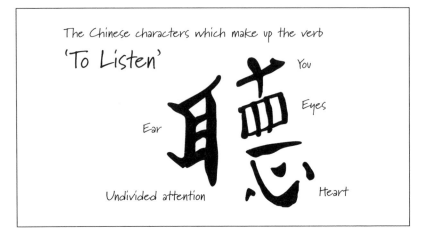

The Chinese characters which make up the verb

'To Listen'

You

Eyes

Ear

Undivided attention

Heart

Listening is our primary source of information from the tutee. It is crucial that we listen, not only for information but also for the emotional clues which accompany this information. Listening for and being sensitive to the affective domain of the tutees concerns will help us have a deeper comprehension of their perception of the situation they are in.

Often, other people's concerns are difficult for us to appreciate as the issues they are facing may have never troubled us. This factor could lead us to diminishing or belittling them and their concerns. However, if we can listen to the emotions and dilemmas beneath their issues, we are offered a deeper layer of human experiencing with which to identify and which may lead us to better understand their predicament.

To listen well requires that we are able to temporarily put aside our own pre-occupations and our own "busyness". Practice in listening skills is strongly encouraged, especially in training situations where you may receive feedback upon your performance.

> "It is as though he listened and such listening as his enfolds us in a silence in which at last we begin to hear what we are meant to be."
> Lao Tzu

UNDERSTANDING / EMPATHY

Sympathy, an emotional facility we have from over-identifying with or feeling sorry for the other person is often not a helpful response to others in need. Our own feelings, evoked by the difficulty this other person is describing may get in the way of us being of assistance to them.

By contrast, the attempt to understand another person, as if one were them, can be most useful in guiding your responses to them. Empathic (or understanding) responses to others provide further proof to them of your acceptance of them as well as the reassurance that they are understandable, they are not unintelligent or crazy. To sense that someone deeply understands you is immensely relieving and releasing.

To attempt to understand another, then, as if one were them, is a core component in the helping process. The 'as if' condition mentioned above is of immense importance as it ensures that you do not become lost in the others dilemma. To understand another and to demonstrate that understanding in your verbal response has a powerful and releasing effect upon them.

PARAPHRASING

Paraphrasing briefly what the student is saying can be an aspect of the empathic process. Also through hearing again what they have said, tutees have the possibility of objectifying their statements and of modifying them towards greater accuracy if they do not sound just right.

There may be circumstances where tutees have never spoken about certain concerns ever before and therefore will not have ready made recipes of words and phrases to describe their dilemma.

Paraphrasing thus offers the opportunity of testing their experienced reality with words they have used to describe that reality.

QUESTIONING

"In order to know well one must be patient in asking questions"

In order to know well, one must be patient in ...asking questions

(from 'Mandarin made Easy'. Pederen)

Many people believe that the central skill in helping is that of questioning. Astute questions delivered with the incisiveness of the interrogator will reveal all, or so the belief goes.

Obviously questions are one potent method for 'finding things out'. However, who needs to find out? And to what end?

This latter question underlies the very model of helping or educating by which one is operating. If the assumption is "I am the educator, therefore I know, therefore I will tell you", then you use questions principally to elicit the information you require in order to give the most accurate response to the student.

If however, you operate upon an educational model that values the role of stimulator or mentor then your questions will be geared to enhancing the students own thinking about their situation.

However, neither model is as simple or as discrete as implied above. Notwithstanding, the nature of the questions emerging are likely to be different in style and form.

In simple terms, one may describe questions as open or closed.

Closed questions ask for specific information which often reflects the needs of the person who has asked:

e.g. "How many 'A' levels have you got?"

Answer: "Four"

Sometimes the tutor will require very specific information in order to advise or help the student and as such closed or specific questions are very legitimate.

However, the skilled use of open questions can be immensely useful in helping the person clarify, through talking, their own position and of course offers the tutor a wider context for their own understanding.

e.g. "I wonder if you could tell me a bit about your 'A' levels".

"Yes, well, I managed to get four, though one of them was only a scrape. However, it was mathematics and I know that was not my strongest subject and by then I also knew that I did not need it to get in here. I therefore did not revise as hard for that one."

Questions can be used quite inappropriately to probe and to persuade. It is suggested that within the tutorial relationship these are not legitimate uses.

HELPFUL AND UNHELPFUL RESPONSES - EXAMPLES

"I'm, really fed up with the landlord. He won't sort out the drains and when I try to speak to him on the 'phone he just puts the 'phone down."

Examples of probably helpful responses

1. Reflection or Paraphrase e.g. "You're saying you're most upset about his refusal to talk to you ..."

2. Open ended questions e.g.

    "Could you say more about this?"

    "How do you feel about this?"

    "What would you like to happen next?"

Here the person has scope to open up and develop what is important for them.

Some specific questions can be helpful if they are following on from open-ended questions and presented as 'checking out' rather than interrogating e.g.:

"It sounds as if there are quite mixed feelings about this?"

"You seem quite tense when talking about 'x' is that difficult for you?"

Examples of probably unhelpful responses

1. **Closed or specific questions** e.g.

"When did this happen?"

"Where is your house?"

Here the person is likely to feel 'probed' or analysed if carried out to excess.

2. **"Why" questions** e.g. "Why did you use the phone?"

"Why are you upset?"

Here the person is likely to feel defensive or guilty and that they can only give explanations rather than explore the issues and feelings.

SUMMARISING

Summarising, from time to time, through the tutorial interview and at the end can provide a helpful indication of accurate understanding for both tutor and tutee: e.g. "We've been talking for a while now and I would like to sum up where we have got to. It seems that you've said that this situation is caused by the following factors ... that have left you feeling .... and as a result your concentration in lectures has been impaired and relationships with your friends have deteriorated. Now you find yourself in a situation which seems difficult to see a way out of, is that right?

Summarising both helps you to check your own understanding as well as helps the students clarify and focus the difficulties described. Also, it is helpful to note and point out discrepancies or apparent contradictions in what has been said, thus highlighting any areas of conflict for the student.

BEING YOURSELF

For many reasons associated with our upbringing, our role, our self-esteem and so on, we can easily rely on standardised or prescriptive responses to a whole range of people and situations. Sometimes such responses are not genuine but are rather compositions of how you think you ought to respond, as a tutor, in this situation.

From the point of view of someone being helped they need to know that what they are being told is a genuine response to them, not necessarily the "party line" or the department's policy. If we are saying one thing and thinking or believing another, this dissonance is often observable and discernible. Questions of your trustworthiness therefore will arise in the student's mind.

Obviously there will be times when institutional policy, for example, will have to be interpreted to the student in order for them to make appropriate decisions. However, such information may be offered as just that, information. If such data is used as a mask to what you feel about the situation then a certain dishonesty occurs in the relationship.

This concept is a particularly difficult one in practice and there are many aspects of it that require much thought and discussion. It is sufficient to say that the student needs to know they are being dealt with in a 'straight' manner.

One aspect of being genuine is that of being able to sensitively and skilfully use **confrontation**. Similar to questioning, confrontation can be used well and productively or at worst as a sledgehammer that only serves to crush and hurt.

Confrontation demands the capacity for being brutally honest without being brutal. The capacity to say the unsayable in a manner that can be heard by the student (rather than defended from) and that does not lead the student to doubt your intention to help is a very considerable skill.

CONSIDERING CHOICES

Towards the end of a personal tutorial, it can be appropriate to explore, with the student, some possible courses of action they might take towards resolving their difficulty. In some cases very little may be possible to achieve other than perhaps arranging to see them again or referring them elsewhere.

However, there will be some situations where a joint brain-storm of ideas, perhaps recorded on paper, might give the student a basis for deciding which of each resolution to take.

Arranging a follow up meeting to assess progress can also be helpful.

IN SUMMATION

In general, avoid the temptation to take control and give advice. It denotes a failure to be empathic. It is what you would do in the student's position and is not appropriate. It also prevents the student from developing his /her own resources to cope with the problem.

Some students need more help than others to develop the level of self-esteem which is essential to problem solving. They usually have the required intellectual ability (demonstrated by their fulfilling the entry requirements) but may lack the emotional maturity or experience. This maturity can be fostered by the personal tutoring relationship.

PERSONAL COMMUNICATION STYLES

SOME PITFALLS

The following examples of styles of communication are included to assist your own personal awareness in reflection upon the ways you communicate. Many of these stylistic conventions, if over-used or inappropriately used will have negative impact upon those you are trying to help.

The list of pitfalls and illustrative text has been freely adapted from an original idea by Jean Brookes, Head of Department of Community Education at the Manchester College of Building.

1. Imposing One's Own values on the Student

There are as many different value stances as there are people, and the tutor's stance is not necessarily any more valid than the student's. It is easier, however, for the tutor to judge the student in terms of his or her own value stance than it is to take time to explore the way the student sees the world...

Example A

Student: "I just can't cope, everything is getting on top of me - there's no point to anything..."

Tutor: "Now, now... pull yourself together. What you need is good night's sleep..."

Example B

Student: "I'm pregnant and..."

Tutor: "What about the father?... when will you be getting married?"

Student: "He doesn't know, and I don't want to get married I..."

Tutor: "Oh no'. Surely you should..."

Student: "Look, I came here to ask you about leave of absence..."

Examples A and B both illustrate the way in which the tutor's imposition of his/her own values can get in the way of the student's needs. The skills this relates to are those of 'attending' and 'suspending value judgements'.

2. Being Over-psychological: Imagining One is able to be Incredibly Insightful

It is all too easy to believe that students can be helped by unsolicited insights. There is a danger in tutors seeing themselves as 'amateur' psychologists, which often implies a need to feel superior, and is shown by the use of inappropriate questions and interpretations, often related to childhood or environment.

Example C

Student: "I am not sure what I should do next... after this course has ended..."

Tutor: "Have you had these feelings of insecurity before?"

Student: "Well, I suppose so... I haven't really thought about it.."

Tutor: "It may well be that as a child you were left alone a lot - did your mother work, ... you arrived home - there was no-one there... the future looked insecure. Yes, I can see why you are afraid."

Students need to retain their own defences and to be allowed to grow at their own pace. To have such interpretations thrust at them is neither helpful nor appropriate. Indeed in unskilled hands they are unlikely to be correct. Any inferences should be drawn with care, and tested out with the students. The skills this relates to is the 'observing' skills of 'making inferences' .

3. Being too Busy to Listen

It is important to give time to a student. If the tutor is too busy, then it is preferable to make an appointment for a time when attention can be give, rather than to press on regardless and hope that the student's difficulty will not be too complex.

Example D

Student: "I just came to see you about my work... I seem to be getting into trouble all the time now..."

Tutor: "Yes, I see" (it's nearly 5 o'clock and the tutor has an appointment at the dentist at 5.15).

Student: "Well .. it's like this... my father..."

Tutor: "Yes?"

Student: "Well... he..."

Tutor: "Look, I'm sorry, but I'll have to go - can you come back tomorrow?"

In Example D, the tutor knew at the beginning of the session that there was no time for anything other than a cursory question and answer. Instead of opening statement "Yes, I see", it would have been more appropriate to use the closing statement "Look I'm sorry..." This would have effectively prevented the student from having twice to try to embark on what is, possibly, a very painful and difficult story. The skills this relates to is that of 'listening '.

4. Finding a Quick Solution

This is often related to a failure to see that there is a real difficulty lying behind the presenting problem, or to a fear of what such a difficulty might be.

Example E

Student: "I can't pay for the field trip next week - my dad's out of work and my mum needs all the money I can send her. If this goes on, I'm going to have to leave and get a job"

Tutor: "Ah well... I think the best thing is to borrow some money out of the welfare fund so you don't miss out on the trip... then you can pay us back next week - that will solve the problem!"

Thus the student in example E is likely to end up with an additional problem of how to repay the money, and is certainly no nearer to identifying and resolving the real issues. The skills this relates to is that of 'responding to content'.

5. Blocking the Student's Emotions

Perhaps because of difficulty in dealing with emotional outbursts, or anxiety about being used as 'punchbag', the tutor may attempt to present what is likely to be the most healthy reaction to a distressing situation - discharge of emotion - by crying, laughing etc.

Example F

Student: "I just can't cope... everything is going wrong... I'm not good at work... I always seem to be in trouble... no-one ever asks me out..."

Tutor: "Now, now, dear... don't cry... pull yourself together: you will be okay... everything will be fine..."

In example F, the student may need to cry before it will be possible to deal rationally with his or her concerns. To block the discharge in the way the tutor is trying to do is likely to increase the student's frustration with the whole situation, including the tutor. The skills this relates to is that of 'responding to feeling'.

6. Asking too many Questions

Often, due to anxiety to do the best for the student, the tutor falls into the trap of asking question after question, thereby constructing a story of his or her making rather then the story the student wanted to tell.

Example G

Student: "I am worried about money"

Tutor: "Aren't you budgeting properly? Do you need to ask for a loan to tide you over? Do your parents help you at all?"

Student   "..."

The most appropriate response to example G would probably be to ask a very open question such as "In what way?" which would allow the student to expand on the theme presented. Instead, by asking so many questions, the tutor is likely to confuse the student. The skills related to this is that of 'questioning'.

7. Wanting to be liked by the Student

In attempting to maintain a sound working relationship with a student, it is all too easy to fall into the trap of feeling indispensable. The danger is that the tutor becomes as dependent on the student as the student may be on the tutor.

Example H

Student: "It is really nice being able to talk to you like this... Nobody understands me like you do... I wish you were my... would you give me your home 'phone number so that I can ring you when I get lonely... perhaps you would come round for a drink some-time."

Tutor: "Oh that's good of you... I'm glad to be able to help you... that's what I'm here for, you know... my 'phone number is... ring any time."

It is vital for the tutor's own mental health to put boundaries around his or her work with students. Example H clearly steps outside such boundaries, the tutor is being drawn into the student's problem, rather than helping the student to confront it. The skills that this relates to is that of 'awareness of emotional attachment'

8.   Not being able to cope with Silence

The tutor often needs to extend his or her existing silence threshold - i.e., ability to comfortably sustain silence - for during such periods the student is often working particularly productively. Unfortunately, many people have low toler-ance of silence.

Example I

Student: "I'm not sure I can take much more... (pause)... I"

Tutor: "Oh come on - it can't be as bad as all that - you're young, things always seem worse than they really are!'

Example J

Student: "I'm not sure I can take much more ... (pause) ... I just don't seem to get on with my parents... (pause)... they have never really understood me, but now it's getting worse... (long pause)... last night... it was awful!"

In example I the tutor is attempting to reassure,, but reassure who - the student or the tutor? The student needs to be allowed to hesitantly put experiences, thoughts and feelings into his or her own words at his or her own pace. The skills that this relates to are those of 'managing silence' and of 'appropriately timing and pacing'.

9. Attempting to Identify too closely with the student

In order to impress the student with the knowledge that the tutor is also human, and has experienced similar difficulties to those of the student, it is all too easy to give an inappropriate response.

Example K

Student: "I've got this girlfriend who's great... my parents are furious because she's white and they say I can't see her any more... we want to get engaged and leave home..."

Tutor: "I know exactly what you mean... when I was your age a very similar thing happened to me... my girlfriend was of a different religion, and my parents disapproved..."

No one person can know exactly how another person feels about anything. There may be clues provided by similarities to one's own experience, but each person's experience of events is unique to him or her, and to make assertions which implicitly deny this is unhelpful. the skills related to this pitfall is that of 'responding'.

10. Wanting to do too much for the Student

Many people feel that, to be helpful to another person, it is important to do things for them, rather than to find ways of helping them do things for themselves.

Example L

Student: "I haven't any money and need some new jeans"

Tutor: "Oh, I'll lend you some money"

Student: "Thanks - it's all so depressing, not being able to get a job"

Tutor: "Look, I know someone who's looking for an assistant - I'll fix it for you"

Student: "…and I've lost my boyfriend…"

Tutor: "I'll take you to the disco tomorrow…"

In Example L, the student needs to be supported so that she can make some decisions and take some actions on her own behalf. The 'I'll fix it' stance of the tutor might make him feel good, but it will not help the student in the long run. The skills this relates to is that of 'target-setting'.

11. Transferring one's own anxiety to the Student

In tutorial work, tutors are likely to be faced with situations that are in some way threatening, especially where the student talks, say, about another member of staff with whom the tutor has a 'difficult' relationship.

Example M.

Student: "I just can't go back to that seminar… each time I go the lecturer picks on me… I can't do anything right, I was wondering if you could go and talk to him about it - I want to do well, but…"

Tutor: "Er… that's Mr. J, isn't it… er… you have to stand on your own feet you know…"

In Example M, the tutor succeeds in adding to the student's anxiety, diminishing the changes that the situation can be rationally discussed and a decision taken. The skills that this pitfall relates to is that of 'immediacy'.

12. Making too many allowances for the student's way of Life

In order to maintain a sound relationship, some tutors make too many allowances for the student, even to the extent of condoning an illegal act for example, and offer confidentiality without any boundaries.

Example N

(After some discussion...)

Student: "...So last night me and some mates got really smashed"

Tutor: "What do you mean by 'smashed'?"

Student: "We had quite a bit to smoke"

Tutor: "Why do you do that?"

Student: "It's something to do, isn't it - there's nothing else to do around here."

Tutor: "No, I suppose not..."

In the emotive issue presented in example N, the tutor has tacitly condoned the actions of the student, and has not indicated any disapproval or indeed pointed out the illegality of his or her actions: this is a dangerous path to tread. The skills that this relates to is that of 'confrontation'.

Note

In each of these pitfalls illustrated above, the intentions of the tutor have not been questioned. Intentions, however, cannot be known by others: they can only be assumed or inferred. It is only the behaviour of the tutor that can be explored and changed.

The above section is modified from Miller J.C., 1983

Other Blocks to Communication

Ordering	Moralising	Offering solutions
Directing	Preaching	Probing
Praising	Reassuring	Questioning
Buttering up	Teaching	Criticism
Warning	Lecturing	Judging
Threatening	Psycho-analysing	Sarcasm
Name calling	Advising	Humour

They have 'YOU' component.

May make people feel guilty.

May communicate lack of respect for the other person.

May cause reactive or retaliatory behaviour.

Can produce resistance rather than openness to change.

May be damaging to the recipient's self-esteem.

May make a person feel hurt and later resentful.

From Gordon, T. 1980

10. GUIDELINES
FOR E-MAIL USAGE

INTRODUCTION

Electronic communication is fast becoming a normal medium for information flow between tutors and students.

Many academic departments now provide a range of standard handouts and texts on computers for their students. These are often formal documents, having been composed using standard English prose.

However, the norms now applying to electronic mail communication have dramatically modified traditional styles of writing. Brevity and spontaneity have become the operating principles, this adding considerably to the efficiency of message transmission. There are accompanying risks inevitably courted by these principles. They include spelling mistakes, lack of punctuation, and such extreme brevity that the message is not understandable to the receiver! This medium also seems to offer the opportunity for ill considered expressions of feelings that might never take place in face to face circumstances. Tutors tempted to fire off strong criticisms on students work have the potential to severely shake the confidence of students concerned. The psychological impact of critical words on the screen unaccompanied by modifying non-verbal behaviour (which is the normal occurrence in all face to face interactions) can be extremely hurtful and a threat to self esteem.

The following extract was originally written from a business management perspective, modified to apply to the Higher Education sector.

It is hoped that the following guidelines will be helpful in your electronic communication with students.

Golden Rules - When Communicating with Groups of Students - (Tutor groups, year groups, special options, interest groups etc.)

● Orientate new group members;

    a) with a welcome.

    b) offer guidelines for the expected procedures.

● Make expectations clear.

● Publish lecture timetables/outlines, bibliographies.

● Publish task assignments - titles, word length, date of completion etc.

● Offer opportunities for consultation/tutorials/supervision.

Helpful Attitudes

● Assume that all students and staff in the organisation are intelligent and well-meaning.

● Assume that members of the group will be able to work together constructively, as long as they make conscious effort to do so.

● Assume that other people's motives are at least as wholesome as yours, until you have incontrovertible evidence to the contrary.

● Recognise that diversity in perspectives and style can if properly, handled, result in a more comprehensive understanding of situations and in more creative solutions.

● Remember that issues come and go, but the people you are working with may be around for a long time into the future. While you may now find yourself in disagreement with someone on Issue A, you might agree on Issue C when it comes up later on.

Helpful Practices

● Follow the conventional guidelines of **e-mail etiquette.**

● Take care to write **e-mail messages that are as clear and concise as possible**. This requires, at the outset, having a reason to write a message in the first place!

● If you write an e-mail message in indignation or in anger, **do not send it**. Delete it, print it out for your own reading, or store it for later reference, but do not send it. In her report on "Productive Behaviours of Global Business Teams", Dianne Hofner Sapphire says that many people interviewed for her study "reported instances when they had reacted too quickly or too emotionally, only to regret it later and were unable to retract the computer note."

● **Respect confidences**. Forward e-mail messages to other people only with the consent of the message's author.

● Before you send any e-mail note, ask yourself, "Would my mother be proud of me for sending this note?" and "**Would I read this aloud from a podium**"?

● **Do your part**. Let others know they can rely on you to do at least your share of the group's work.

● **Suspend judgement**. Make sure you understand what others are saying before you respond to them. Seek clarification whenever you have any doubt as to someone's meaning or intention.

● **Try to understand**. Not just other people's ideas, but their situations as well. How much pressure are they under? What competing demands or ideas do they face?

● **Spell out the assumptions** on which your viewpoints or suggestions are based.

● If you raise an objection to someone else's idea or suggestion try to **suggest alternatives**.

● If you have a criticism of another's efforts, **offer to help**.

● If you give offence or fail to fulfil a commitment, **apologise**. Without offering excuses.

From: Althen, G. (1997) NAFSA Newsletter. February. p.31

11. PAINFUL MOMENTS IN TUTORING

DELIVERING BAD NEWS

At some time in any career in higher education there will occur moments when you are expected as a staff member to do something for which you are not prepared. Part of the complexity of an academic career is that you play so many different roles for a large group of people regardless of the particular role you may want to emphasise yourself.

When it comes to telling someone that a parent or adult child has died there are no 'right' ways to proceed or to avoid the pain and powerlessness with which you will be in touch. However you can make sure you give yourself and the other person time and privacy. If it is possible to ensure that someone else can be there when you have to withdraw your own support it can be helpful. Even the most experienced of counsellors have to wipe away a tear or two when dealing with bereavement so don't expect yourself to be able to maintain total composure. Needless to say the bereft person should not be troubled or burdened with your feelings but neither do you have to disguise yourself with an impenetrable mask.

Sometimes bad news is met with disbelief or shock and even denial - give the other person a chance to really grasp the message. Nothing you say or do is going to change the awful fact of a death so avoid trying to make it better by uttering platitudes. When you have to leave the person for whatever reason be aware of your own need to soothe the anxiety and loss that any contact with death brings. Each person has his or her own unique style of responding to such needs. Don't make the mistake of thinking that everyone will respond like you but do respect your own needs in situations such as this. Make sure too that those other members of staff in the department who will need to know what has happened are informed in a sensitive manner.

It may be useful to remember in the weeks and months that follow that the normal process of grieving over the loss of a close relationship can take up to and beyond two years. There are phases in this mourning in which people can get stuck but generally speaking we tend to have forgotten in this country how to manage this period, and try to rush people on too quickly to getting back to 'normal'. There are great cultural and religious differences about what is considered appropriate in relation to grief and the rituals involved. If you are in doubt about any aspect of mourning you may want to consider having a chat with a chaplain or a counsellor.

COPING WITH SUDDEN BEREAVEMENT

Someone you know may have died. Your experience was a very personal one but this pamphlet will help you know how others have reacted in similar situations. It will also show how you can help normal healing to occur and to avoid some pitfalls.

Normal Feelings and Emotions Often Experienced

Fear
- of damage to one self and those we love.
- of being left alone, of having to leave loved ones.
- of breaking down or losing control.
- of a similar event happening again.

Helplessness
- crisis shows up human powerlessness, as well as strength.

Sadness
- for your friend's/relative's death.

Longing
- for all that has gone.

Guilt
- for being better off than others, i.e. being alive, regrets for things not done.

Shame
- for having been exposed as helpless, 'emotional' and needing others, for not having reacted as one would have wished.

Anger
- at what has happened, at whoever caused it or allowed it to happen.

- at the injustice and senselessness of it all.

- at the shame and indignities.

- at the lack of proper understanding by others, the inefficiencies.

- WHY ME?

Memories
- of feeling, of loss of love for other people in your life who have been injured or died.

Let down
- disappointment, which alternates with...

Hope
- for the future, for better times.

Everyone has these feelings. The experience of other accidents has shown that they may be particularly intense if:

deaths were sudden, violent, or occurred in horrifying circumstances

there was great dependence on the person who died

the relationship with the person was at a difficult stage.

Nature heals through allowing these feelings to come out. This will not lead to loss of control of the mind, but stopping these feelings may lead to nervous and physical problems. Crying gives relief.

PHYSICAL AND MENTAL SENSATIONS

You may feel bodily sensations with or without the feelings described. Sometimes they are due to the crisis, even if they develop many months after the event.

Some common sensations are tiredness, sleeplessness, bad dreams, fuzziness of the mind including loss of memory and concentration, dizziness, palpitations, shakes, difficulty in breathing, choking in the throat and chest, nausea, diarrhoea, muscular tension which may lead to pain, e.g. headaches, neck and backaches, dragging in the womb, menstrual disorders, change in sexual interest.

FAMILY AND SOCIAL RELATIONSHIPS

New friendships and group bonds may come into being. On the other hand, strains in relationships may appear. The good feelings in giving and receiving may be replaced by conflict. You may feel that too little or the wrong things are offered, or that you cannot give as is expected.

Accidents are more frequent after severe stresses. Alcohol and drug intake may increase due to the extra tensions.

THE FOLLOWING MAKE THE EVENTS AND FEELINGS ABOUT THEM EASIER TO BEAR.

Numbness

● Your mind may allow the misfortune to be felt slowly. At first you may feel numb. The event may seem unreal, like a dream, something that has not really happened. People often see this wrongly either as 'being strong', or 'uncaring'.

Activity

● To be active. To help and give to others may give some relief.

However, over-activity is detrimental if it diverts attention from the help you need for yourself.

Reality

● Confronting this reality, e.g. attending the funeral, inspecting losses, returning to the scene, will all help you to come to terms with the event.

Allowing the feelings

● As you allow the disaster more into your mind, there is a need to think about it, to talk about it, and at night to dream about it over and over again.

Support

● It is a relief to receive other people's physical and emotional support. Do not reject it. Sharing with others who have had similar experiences feels good. Barriers can break down and closer relationships develop.

Privacy   ● In order to deal with feelings, you will find it
                       necessary at times to be alone, or just with family
                       and close friends.

                       Activity and numbness (blocking of feelings) may be
                       overused and may delay your healing.

Healing   ● Remember that the pain of the wound leads into
                       healing. You may even come out wiser and stronger.

SOME DO'S AND DONT'S

Don't bottle up feelings. **Do** express your emotions.

Don't avoid talking about what happened. **Do** take every opportunity to review the experience within yourself and with others. **Do** allow yourself to be part of a group of people who care.

Don't let your embarrassment stop you giving others the chance to talk.

Don't expect the memories to go away - the feelings will stay with you for a long time to come.

Do take time out to sleep, rest, think and be with your close family and friends.

Do express your needs clearly and honestly to family, friends and officials.

Do try to keep your lives as normal as possible after the acute grief.

Do drive more carefully, do be more careful around the home and on campus.

Warning: Accidents are more common after severe stresses - do try to take more care with everyday activities.

WHEN TO SEEK PROFESSIONAL HELP

1. If you feel you cannot handle intense feeling or body sensations.

   If you feel that your emotions are not falling into place over a period of time, you feel chronic tensions, confusion, emptiness or exhaustion.

   If you continue to have body symptoms.

2. If after a month you continue to feel numb and empty and do not have the appropriate feelings described. If you have to keep active in order not to feel.

3. If you continue to have nightmares and poor sleep.

4. If you have no person or group with whom to share your emotions and you feel the need to do so.

5. If your relationships seem to be suffering badly, or sexual problems develop.

6. If you have accidents.

7. If you continue to smoke, drink, or take drugs to excess since the event.

8. If your work performance suffers.

9. If you note that those around you are particularly vulnerable or are not healing satisfactorily.

10. If as a helper you are suffering 'exhaustion'.

● **Do remember that you are basically the same person that you were before the accident**

● **Do remember that there is a light at the end of the tunnel**

● **Do remember that if you suffer too much or too long, help is available.**

WHERE TO SEEK PROFESSIONAL HELP

University Counselling Service
Mushroom Lane
Sheffield S10 2TS
Tel (0114) 222 4134

University Health Service
2, Claremont Place
Sheffield S10 2TB
Tel (0114) 276 9447

Cruse-Bereavement Care
69 Division Street
Sheffield
Tel (0114) 272 5797

This extract is based on a leaflet produced by the University of Birmingham, and reproduced with their permission.

STUDENT ILLNESS

Two very good booklets on health matters are:

a) What Should I Do? Student/Young Persons Guide

b) What Should I Do? Do I go to the doctors?
Publisher: RTFB Publishing Ltd.
                    Building Z
                    Shamrock Quay
                    Southampton SO14 5QL
                    Tel: 01703 229041
                    Fax: 01703 227274

Both booklets offer descriptions of familiar ailments, illnesses and conditions with suggestions for self-care management where appropriate. These are useful texts both for the tutors own resources as well as for students.

Other matters relating to student illness are most appropriately referred to the:

University Health Service
2, Claremont Place
Sheffield S10 2TB
Tel (0114) 276 9447

DISCIPLINARY PROBLEMS

Regulations and rules enable all of us to feel we know what is required of us and where the limits lie in terms of behaviour. We can enforce regulations in a firm way without resort to put-downs and attacks on character. If a student transgresses in some way he or she needs to be given a clear idea of what has gone wrong, what can be rescued from a bad situation (if anything can be rescued) and what the consequences are if unacceptable behaviour continues. Fudging and prevarication can make a difficult situation worse. It is sometimes helpful to think about giving criticism of any kind as an educational endeavour requiring tact and firmness and to keep in mind the notion that saying no and rejecting someone's behaviour is not the same as rejecting the person. Be clear in your own mind and you will feel more comfortable with the student. Do make sure you have got all your facts straight and that other members of staff will be taking the same approach. It may be useful to keep a record for yourself of what you have requested from someone and when.

The rules and regulations of the University are available from the Registrar's Department.

WHAT TO DO WHEN A STUDENT SEEMS TO BE MENTALLY DISTURBED

From time to time some students will experience such stress and pressure that they develop mental health problems and demonstrate untypical or disturbing behaviour. The purpose of this section is to help you to recognise when help is necessary, to know what to do and who to tell.

STUDENT COUNSELLORS AND OTHER AGENCIES

During the course of university life, the majority of students who experience problems in their lives which cause them some distress will find a way of coping for themselves or find their own way to the University Counselling Service or University Health Service. Tutor's awareness and acknowledgement that students require support, encouragement and rehearsal can minimise the impact of dealing with assignment deadlines, meeting new people and having to become an independent learner. For example, when students are asked to present their own research, ideas and thoughts to others in the form of a presentation, it can raise their fears to levels of crippling anxiety, incapacity or withdrawal.

Other members of staff on the campus are only likely to become involved in extreme cases where the student noticeably begins to disrupt the day to day routine. It might be important to emphasise that many problems may not be as serious as they might at first seem, although panic, anxiety, depression, phobias, eating disorders and the like can be very real, scary and disabling to the person concerned.

It is not always necessary to involve outside agencies, and, in any event, all students would be offered confidential assistance by the Counselling Service and University Health Service, unless it is felt that they were likely to be an immediate danger to themselves or others. At these times the University Counsellors and Doctors will, where necessary and appropriate, work in co-operation with other General Practitioners, Social Workers, Psychiatrists, Psychologists and Community Psychiatric Nurses in Community Mental Health teams

1. WHAT IS NORMAL?

It might be helpful to recognise a distinction between 'neuroses' and 'psychoses'.

Neuroses is the name given to more common, less serious, types of discomforting personal experience and behaviour. These include panic attacks, anxiety, phobias, depression, obsessions and compulsions. They can be very disturbing to the person concerned but are distinguished from more serious mental illnesses (psychoses) by the person's ability to know that something is wrong and to worry about it.

Psychoses refers to those illnesses where the sufferer experiences, at times, such severe distress that he or she loses touch with reality completely. People with psychotic disturbances often aren't aware that anything is wrong and are unlikely to seek help. Examples of psychotic conditions are schizophrenia and manic depression.

It is said that individuals with neuroses add 2 + 2 and make 4 but worry about it. Whereas individuals with psychoses say 2 + 2 = 5 and that's OK!

People rarely get through their lives without experiencing difficulties, some of which are so intense and confusing that the subsequent stress will result in changes of mood and behaviour. Many people will cope with these times by themselves, and in their own way, perhaps without colleagues and friends having knowledge of their difficulties.

It is sometimes difficult to identify individuals who may be experiencing problems. Sensitivity is often required because of an individual's reluctance initially to either admit to themselves that they have problems, or, to disclose the fact to others. It may feel even more daunting without the support of tried and trusted friends and family.

There will be students with anxiety and stress related problems who will complete their studies successfully. Some will need the help of counsellors or other professional services in order to solve their particular difficulty. Some students will have even more serious difficulties and will still be able to complete their courses, although the occurrence of a 'life-changing' difficulty towards the end of the academic year usually has a more disruptive effect upon the student's academic performance because of the shortage of time available for recovery relative to course deadlines. The advice and support of academic staff can often minimise the added stress for individuals on such occasions.

It is important not to stereotype or label people with mental health problems. Most are not dangerous or troublesome, anymore than people who are physically unwell. Remember that recognising 'abnormality' means firstly defining what is 'normal'. What is considered acceptable in one family, country, civilisation or period of history may be considered bizarre in the extreme in another. Being different culturally, sexually or socially is not being abnormal or ill. Doing something different from the norm or living a socially unacceptable life-style does not constitute mental illness.

2. WHEN IS HELP NEEDED? POSSIBLE INDICATORS

Occasionally you will come into contact with students who have become so disturbed by internal and external pressures that the resulting distress is affecting their lives. In these circumstances you may need to find help for them.

If a student seems to be experiencing delusions, hallucinations or hearing voices, and seems to be out of touch with reality over a period of time, it may be that the person is suffering from a mental illness. Other behaviours which point in this direction could include making threats and accusations, alleging persecution, irrational mood swings and/or talking as several people. At this stage, it may be helpful to ask someone who knows the student fairly well whether that student's behaviour is significantly different.

Be specially watchful for somebody whose speech is racing or jumping from one subject to another, someone who believes that people are out to get him or her and, for example, may describe thought rays or voices inside the head and suggests you should whisper. People may be deluded, think they are somebody else or have somebody else inside them. They may talk to inanimate objects. They may hear voices and sometimes you may hear them conducting a conversation alone but in different voices. In these latter situations, the person may need professional help quickly. Obtain help but do not panic and do not jump to conclusions, there may be other reasons for the behaviour.

Although it may be extremely unnerving or frightening to deal with behaviour which you perceive as bizarre, antisocial, aggressive or unpredictable, they do not, per se, constitute evidence of mental illness, and neither does behaviour influenced by drugs or alcohol. A student will need to be challenged about this kind of behaviour through the procedures outlined in the Student Regulations, as would be the case for any other incident. However threatening the behaviour might be, General Practitioners or the Police will be unlikely to attend unless the person presents an immediate danger, either to himself/herself or others.

Do remember that people do not lose their rights as adults if they become ill. A student may not want their parents or spouse to know that there is a problem. Confidentiality is very important in these situations and deciding when confidentiality has to be breached for the well-being of the student is an important judgement that sometimes has to be made.

3. WHAT TO DO

There is no real substitute for talking, so if you are worried about a student, talk to them and if you still feel concerned, suggest that they see a Student Counsellor, Doctor or some other professional helper. If you believe they are losing touch with reality and it is difficult to talk with them, you will need to make a referral for them.

The appropriate action in these situations is to contact the student's G.P., who will then arrange for an approved Social Worker or a Psychiatrist to see the student and to make an assessment. Depending on the outcome of the assessment, a student might then be taken into hospital or stabilised through the use of medication, the latter often enabling the student to continue to study.

A GP might not necessarily be able to immediately attend to a student, even if his or her behaviour is very disruptive. It might just be suggested that you escort the student to the casualty department of the hospital. Often, mentally ill people find it impossible to recognise their illness or their need for help, which exacerbates the problem.

The counsellors have some experience of working with students who are disturbed and they are very willing to help by offering support or by contacting the appropriate services. However, it should be understood that the counsellors have no more authority than any other member of staff within the institution, to do anything further or to act in any capacity, other than that outlined above.

4. HOSPITAL ADMISSION

In serious cases it may be necessary to arrange for emergency, possibly compulsory, admission to a psychiatric hospital, and this will need the agreement of two doctors and an approved social worker. Obtaining help in acute cases can sometimes be a long and involved business, especially if it is an evening or a weekend. The first course of action is always to call the student's GP. The GP is able to open the door to all the other services. If problems recur after the GP has left, then negotiation and much telephoning may be necessary. You may be helped in this by one of the university counsellors, depending on who is available. If you feel somebody needs help, do not give up - sometimes the red tape of the system needs a lot of working through.

Whereas someone who is mentally ill may be able to continue with or resume studies when treated, it would seem that the course of action for persistent behavioural problems, without an accompanying assessment of mental illness, would be to suspend the student on the grounds that he or she has contravened Student Regulations.

5. AFTER!

After suffering a serious mental health episode, the student may return to the University with much guilt about what they might have said or done while they were unwell and feeling very scared about the possibility of it happening again.

In these circumstances, the student counsellors are available to offer help, support and ongoing therapy. You should ensure that the student is aware of the services available and that they feel able to seek help if things appear to be going wrong. It is important to emphasise that many people will come through an episode of mental illness feeling stronger and more aware of their own strengths and weaknesses. They will be more able to recognise signs of stress earlier in the future, and therefore significantly reduce the chances of problems repeating themselves.

SOME POINTS TO BE AWARE OF:

● The University Health Service, phone no. 0114 276 9477

● Students cannot be forced to receive medical treatment, although it might be possible for them to be suspended with the encouragement of the possibility of their return, once they have sought medical help.

● The counsellors do not have any powers to act, although they can make contacts and do have some expertise in dealing with disturbed students.

● Prompt and clear indications to the student that their behaviour is causing concern is often most helpful, rather than delaying a confrontation, if only from the point of view of the welfare of other students and peace of mind for staff.

● Individuals who experience mental illness are very rarely dangerous and should be spoken to and treated as 'normally' as possible. This approach applies to all communication with disturbed students, including any observations about their condition. A calm response, a quiet area to be in and the offer to spend some time with the person can be the most effective immediate action.

● The legal process of 'Sectioning', i.e. compulsory admittance to psychiatric wards under Section 2 of the Mental Health Act, can only be put in motion by General Practitioners, Approved Social Workers and Psychiatrists. No one else can 'recommend' it. It is used only in extreme cases and exists for fixed time periods. Once a person has been admitted compulsorily to a psychiatric hospital, it remains on his or her medical records permanently.

(The above extract is reprinted with permission from an occasional paper of the same name distributed by the Student Counselling Service, University of Humberside)

DEALING WITH DIFFICULT AND DISRUPTIVE SITUATIONS

Remember difficult and disruptive situations are ones in which your **normal coping strategies don't work**. They are likely to make you feel de-skilled and feel that you don't have the resources to manage them.

Because of this you are **likely to panic**, find yourself **unable to think, act impulsively** or over emotionally and generally in ways you may regret in retrospect.

Because of this, it is likely that **after the event**:

a) you and your colleagues will be able to think of better ways you could have coped with the situation.

b) You and your colleagues are likely to **apportion blame** and try to find out whose fault it was that things went wrong and the situation happened.

This is because difficult and disruptive situations, by definition, are difficult to handle. They often appear chaotic and can give the impression of having been handled "badly".

WAYS OF AVOIDING THIS

● **Anticipation** - it always helps to think about potentially difficult situations in advance and plan, as far as possible, what to do in certain eventualities, e.g. by having departmental meetings to discuss procedures on :

a) discipline problems

b) sudden unexpected violence

c) disturbed or irrational behaviour

d) sudden illness - collapse

e) sexual/racial harassment, homophobic behaviour.

f) uncontrollable arguments

g) threatening/abusive behaviour.

Know your procedures and know who to **report an incident** to - know **who you can call on** for immediate **support**.

Don't feel ashamed of not being able to cope. **Call in assistance**.

● If someone is very upset, angry or difficult, sit them down with a cup of tea or coffee. This will give you time to think. **Don't feel you have to come up with an instant answer.**

● **Try not to join in** with someone who's very angry, **by retaliating**. If someone is insulting you or shouting at you try to comment on this behaviour rather than shouting back - (e.g. "You are obviously very angry"). Keep your emotional distance.

● **Remain firm - try not to show that you are afraid** of a violent or abusive person. Most violent people fear that they will get further out of control and no one will be able to manage them.

● **Don't be afraid to say "no"** if you mean "no". It is tempting to appease people who are being difficult or behaving in a bullying way. Remember they too are frightened of the bullying part of themselves and they need to be **reassured by firmness**.

● Very disturbed or irrational behaviour usually has some meaning. **Try to listen** to what a person is saying behind the apparently illogical.

● **Do not be afraid to state the obvious to a disturbed person**. Tell them that you know they are obviously very upset or very stressed. **Most people fear being direct** and saying what they mean but a straightforward attitude can be a great relief to people in this state.

● Difficult and disruptive situations always leave people feeling stressed, so it is important to find some time to **talk things over** with colleagues afterwards in a supportive, non accusatory way.

● It is important that serious incidents, particularly where people are hurt, **are thoroughly** and **fairly investigated** and procedures are gone through properly. These incidents should not be swept under the carpet. Justice should be seen to be done.

● **Try not to blame yourself or others** after the event. Post mortems are only useful if they help to make you feel more able to cope in future difficult or disruptive situations.

● **There is no right way** to deal with difficult or disruptive situations. What helps, is holding on to your capacity to think and knowing what support systems you have to help you cope as well as possible in these sorts of situations.

● Remember that one thing everyone dreads, when a dealing with a difficult or disruptive situation, is their colleagues or manager telling them they got it wrong. Most people do **the best they can** in these situations and apportioning blame **after** the event creates more anxiety and is likely to inflame the handling of future incidents.

The above extract is reprinted, with permission, from an occasional paper of the same name written by Anne Heyno, Head of the Counselling Service, University of Westminster.

MANAGING STUDENT ANGER

DEALING WITH ANGER, STEP BY STEP

Step 1: Listen to the Angry Student

Helpful Actions

● Acknowledging the anger and sending the message that you understand the student is angry.

● Listening carefully to what the student says. Waiting to respond until the student has had a chance to vent the negative feelings, anger and hostility.

- Keeping an open mind about the problem and the resolution until you have had a chance to investigate the situation and talk with colleagues.

- Remembering that the student is probably seeing the situation from a perspective very different from yours.

Unhelpful Actions

- Denying the student's anger.

- Telling him or her to calm down.

- Telling the student that you refuse to listen because of the anger.

- Telling the student that you do not want to hear the reason for the anger.

- Reacting to the student's anger in a defensive manner when you, your programme, or your institution has been attacked.

Step 2: Help the Student Deal with the Anger

Helpful Actions

- Helping the student save face when he or she realises that behaviour has been inappropriate and embarrassing.

- Helping the student to a private area where he or she can express negative feelings without being observed by others.

- Sitting down with the student, assuring a posture that is relaxed and nonthreatening.

- Speaking in a calm voice at a low pitch.

- Keeping judgements to yourself about what should or should not make people angry.

- Offering support to the student when the anger subsides, without necessarily agreeing.

Unhelpful Actions

- Focussing on the inappropriate, foolish, or bad behaviour

- Engaging in a heated debate in a public area (if others are in the advising area, consider it public).

● Standing while the student is sitting, this sends a message of dominance over the other person.

● Responding to the student's anger by also raising your voice.

● Jumping to conclusions about what should and should not make people angry, and expressing those opinions to the student.

● Taking advantage of the student's calmer state to begin arguing or attacking.

Step 3: Help Yourself Deal with Student's Anger

Helpful Actions

● Asking for assistance from a fellow adviser or trusted colleague if you feel that you can no longer handle the situation or control your own anger.

● Venting your own feelings with someone you trust after the appointment.

Unhelpful Action

● Trying to handle the appointment when you feel that you can no longer remain objective.

● Keeping your feelings to yourself after an emotionally challenging appointment.

The above guidelines are reprinted with permission from Margaret Coffey and Susan Grace Intercultural Advising in English-Language Programs (Washington,D.C. NAFSA 1997). pp.54-55.

12. HARASSMENT AND THE UNIVERSITY HARASSMENT POLICY

Dealing with harassment is stressful for all concerned and may involve the tutor in a complex set of power relations in a similar way to those affecting the victim. Usually people are loathe to proceed with taking action over an allegation because they have little evidence other than their own word to back up the claim. This could mean the word of a student, or junior member of staff against an established figure of authority in the University. The risk to an 'accuser' can seem very high. It is perhaps well to remember comments made earlier in this booklet about the blurring of roles which happens when tutors or other staff become more than friendly with students. Students are always in an unequal power relation to staff however sophisticated either party might feel. Harassment is a serious problem and needs to be addressed. All claims should be taken seriously and confidentiality must be closely guarded. Where permission is given for the matter to be taken up by the University it must still remain a highly confidential matter. Within the university there are specially trained staff who are able to respond by offering a confidential interview and giving advice on how to proceed.

INITIAL STEPS

If you are approached by a student or member of staff who is indicating that s/he has been harassed in any form:

1. Listen carefully without passing judgement on either parties behaviour.

2. Depending on the severity of the allegation, ask the student or member of staff if s/he is able to ask the person/group to stop the offending behaviour.

3. Ask the person if they would like to contact a member of the Universities Harassment Network and provide them with a list of people they can contact. A list of Network members is available from the Student Advice Centre, Academic Departments, Student Services Department, Personnel Department and Counselling Service.

The University has a policy against harassment which includes sexual, racial and other forms of personal harassment. There are clear guidelines for both staff and students on what to do if they experience harassment. Detailed below are the Personal Harassment Procedures, outlining the formal and informal procedures. Additional copies are available from the Student Advice Centre, Student Services Department, Academic Departments, Personnel Department and the Counselling Service.

WHAT IS HARASSMENT?

Personal Harassment is defined as any behaviour which is unacceptable to the recipient and which creates an intimidating, hostile or offensive environment for employment, study or social life. Although harassment is often thought of as an overt use of power, it can also appear in more subtle guises.

The following points are important.

● Anyone can suffer from harassment.

● An action or statement does not have to be repeated over a long period of time to be defined as harassment. A single statement or action may constitute harassment.

● Even behaviour which is not meant to cause offence or distress may do so.

● It is the impact of the words or action, not the underlying intent which is important.

● Health, physical characteristics, personal beliefs and numerous other factors may lead to harassment.

● Harassment can occur between people of the opposite sex or between people of the same sex.

- Differences of culture, language and attitude, or misinterpretation of social signals may mean that what is perceived as offensive behaviour or language by one person may not seem so to another.

It is difficult to categorise all forms of harassment, but examples of some more easily recognisable forms of harassment are listed below.

Sexual Harassment

A form of sex discrimination involving unwanted sexual attention which emphasises sexual status over a person's individual status.

Some examples of sexual harassment are -

- Remarks, looks, jokes, use of offensive language, alluding to a person's private life or sexual orientation by innuendo, or remarks about a person's appearance.

- Making provocative suggestions or pressing people to accept unwelcome invitations.

Racial Harassment

A form of racial discrimination, involving offensive behaviour by a person or group of one racial or ethnic origin against a person or group of another.

Examples of racial harassment include -

- Derogatory name-calling.

- Insults and racist jokes.

- Ridicule of an individual for cultural differences.

- Exclusion from everyday conversation or social events.

- Unfair allocation of work and responsibilities because of racial or ethnic origin.

- Display of offensive, racist material.

Other Forms of Personal Harassment

Harassment may take many forms and people can be subject to harassment on a variety of grounds including sexual orientation, religious or political convictions, age, real or suspected infection with AIDS/HIV, or disability.

Examples include -

● Gibes in reference to personal traits or appearance, invasion of privacy or practical jokes which cause offence.

● Academic bullying - asserting a position of intellectual superiority in an aggressive, abusive or offensive manner, threats of academic failure, public sarcasm.

● Any difficulty in defining personal harassment should not deter a member of staff or student from seeking support or complaining of behaviour which causes them offence or distress.

WHAT TO DO NEXT

If you believe you are being subjected to harassment of any form, you do not have to feel it is your fault and you do not have to tolerate it. Any employee or student who suffers from harassment from any individual or group in the course of their work or study will have the support of the University in seeking to ensure that harassment ceases. There are various ways in which an individual can deal with harassment, ranging from asking the person to stop, to taking up a formal complaint.

Informal Procedure

If possible you should speak to the alleged harasser yourself, making it clear that his/her behaviour is unacceptable and you wish it to stop. In many cases such an approach is successful and the harassment ceases.

You may wish to seek help from a friend, sympathetic colleague or from someone in authority whom you feel able to talk to and who may also accompany you to meetings. This might be your Head of Department, Union representative, Union of Students' Sabbatical Officer or Advice Worker.

You can request a confidential meeting with a member of the University Harassment Network who has been trained to handle problems relating to personal harassment and who will be able to listen and advise you. A list of Network members is available from the Student Advice Centre, Academic Departments, Student Services Department, Personnel Department and Counselling Service.

Formal Procedure

Whilst many situations can be resolved at an informal level, formal action can be taken if the above stages fail to be effective in stopping the harassment or where the behaviour is of such a serious nature that informal measures would be inappropriate.

● Ask for a confidential interview with your Head of Department or with any person from the University Harassment Network. They will listen to you in confidence and give you advice on how to proceed.

● All formal complaints of harassment should, wherever possible, be raised by the complainant with the Head of Department. S/he will consider the nature of the claim, make initial enquiries and take any action deemed appropriate. If discussion with the Head of Department is not possible, or is inappropriate, you should seek advice from a member of the Personal Harassment Network, the Personnel Department (for staff) or the Department of Student Services (for students).

THE POLICY

Harassment of people at work or in the learning environment is a feature of discrimination, which is prohibited by law. The University considers all forms of harassment to be extremely serious and is committed to eliminating harassment experienced by students or staff and will take steps to investigate complaints thoroughly.

It is not possible to set down detailed guidelines as to how every case will be pursued due to the diverse and sensitive nature of harassment issues. Complaints will be dealt with in the strictest confidence and investigations will be carried out impartially.

Formal action may include the University Disciplinary and Grievance procedures for staff and students, copies of which are available from the Departments of Personnel and Student Services respectively. Depending on the nature of the issue, however, the University may decide to take alternative action to the procedures specified for disciplinary or grievance cases.

The complainant will be fully advised of the reasons for any course of action decided on. No action will be taken without his/her knowledge and agreement. If the University decides not to pursue a complainant's claims, s/he will be informed of the alternatives open to her/him. The complainant will always be informed of the final outcome of the action or case.

The policy does not seek to encourage false and unfair accusations of harassment and during all investigations of complaints the alleged harasser will have the opportunity to give a clear account of her/his case and to be represented.

Further copies of this Harassment policy are available from the Student Advice Centre, Student Services Departments, Personnel Department and the Counselling Service.

13. STUDENTS WHO ARE OLDER, CULTURALLY DIFFERENT OR WHO HAVE PARTICULAR NEEDS

Students who are 18 years old and fresh from 'A' levels vary enormously in their expectations, preferences and backgrounds. We tend to lump them together in our minds as a homogeneous, stereotyped group because this makes it easier for us to think quickly about what they need from us and how we can respond to their needs. In a sense, minority groups of students are met with a similar pigeon-holing which allows us rapid access to ideas about adapting our way of relating or teaching. Stereotyping then, can be useful but can also block our view of what the student might really need. If a student is not easily identifiable as having special needs then it is all to easy for him/her to be misunderstood or neglected.

THE 'OLDER' STUDENT

We have avoided using the term 'mature' because it connotes immaturity in younger students which is unfair and suggests that older students have acquired some ephemeral quality which they often feel themselves is lacking. Whatever the age of the older student, at various times, throughout a University career and (sometimes fluctuating between these extremes in one seminar!), s/he will feel both inappropriately childlike and deskilled and at the same time too 'old' and 'different' from the majority.

It is usually after a period of re-evaluation that someone undertakes to enter full-time study. The expenses incurred are high for those who have given up employment and for those whose financial status will be detrimentally affected if they have been receiving unemployment and some other benefits. The further costs emotionally and economically of a degree course are such that a student will not tolerate readily a sense that s/he is falling behind with academic work. Failure can be experienced very sharply given these background circumstances. This makes for a difficult job for personal tutors who have to reassure where appropriate but be clear and demanding about good academic standards. Sometimes older students have arrived on courses after a great deal of personal interaction and encouragement from access tutors and others. It is necessary for them to learn to study in a more impersonal environment and to come to terms with the limits which exist on tutors' availability. The same process must be negotiated by many younger students too but seems to be acutely felt by people who have worked for years with a dream of university life which often fails to turn out as planned.

One particular problem which affects older students is the difficulty in keeping a perspective on the field of knowledge or study that has to be entered for any one piece of work. Trying to read, write or do too much in an academic sense is a temptation for someone who may be passionately interested in his/her subject. Help in setting realistic study goals and clear guidelines about what is required in a piece of work can assist the student immensely. In fact, older students are often more open about their difficulties and may well be alerting tutors to problems in communication or teaching that other students are also experiencing.

Part of the background to registering at university will be a complex denouement of personal and career development needs. Sometimes the impact of being a student is a powerful blow to an already fragile marriage or a family life which fails to nurture. The network of relationships around a student has to be able to alter and adapt to the demands of university life and to what is often the beginnings of a new personality emerging from the old familiar one. If late adolescence had not been a spontaneous and exciting time the first time round it can be revisited with gusto at university causing all sorts of problems as well as releasing creativity and the opportunity to develop. This means that in several ways 'mature' students will be quite vulnerable. We estimate that in the Counselling Service over 40% of our clientele are over the age of 21 at the outset of their courses. Despite the emphasis on negatives, older students can be a 'blessing': , generally speaking, they work very hard and they will probably be the ones who will let you know if they are in trouble or indeed if there is a departmental problem that needs addressing.

● Useful contacts in relation to mature students are:

   a) Elizabeth Hall, Department of Student Services   21268

   b) Mature Students Association, Students' Union   28536

STUDENTS WITH DISABILITES

Students with special needs such as access to particular forms of equipment or whose learning might be affected by mobility, perceptual or communication problems may not pose any other immediate challenge to a tutor. You may merely need to inform yourself of the contacts mentioned after this paragraph and ensure that all that is available to the student in terms of help is forthcoming. However, if you are able to establish a good relationship with a student you may well discover that there are many ways in which you and the department could make small alterations to standard practice which can greatly enhance the experience of university for students as well as helping them to be more successful academically.

Where a student has suffered a recent loss of function there may be all sorts of feelings and self doubt which show themselves in indirect ways. It is sometimes difficult to be fair and optimistic while retaining a sense of the very real limitations a student may be struggling to deal with. It can be helpful to initiate regular meetings where the student can feel invited to seek help rather than have preconceptions imposed on him or her or the equally unhelpful experience of constantly having to go and ask for something from a department and thereby being made to feel inadequate.

The University has a Disability officer whose contact details are published below.

● Marie Norris - Disability and Hardship ext. 21264

● Department of Student Services

● Skill: National Bureau for Students with Disabilities:
336, Brixton Road, London SW9 7AA.
Tel: 0171 274 0565

● University Health Service ext. 22101

DIFFERENT CULTURES, DIFFERENT EXPECTATIONS

"The culture of a particular people or other social body is everything one must learn in order to behave in ways that are recognisable, predictable and understandable to those people."

C.A. Valentine (1968)

"I define culture as a collective mental programming of a people in an environment."

G. Hofstede (1980)

The dynamics of at least of three different cultures impact upon any international student in this country.

They are: (a) their culture of origin

(b) the culture in which they have come to live.

(c) the culture of higher education.

There are, of course, very obvious aspects of culture that can be identified and understood. They will include things such as language, customs, manners, history, folklore and literature. However, aspects of culture we are less aware of will include: communication styles, role expectations, non-verbal communication, order of priorities, patterns of interpersonal relationships, approaches to carrying out tasks, how tasks are assigned, patterns of touch, interpersonal space, observation of time, male-female relations, attitudes towards authority, concepts of individualism or collectivism, and many more.

One of the complexities, then, of living in another culture for a period of time is how to make sense of or learn about this new culture. The residents of the culture seldom teach their ways of being and doing to visitors as they themselves a) do not appreciate necessarily that what they do is culture driven and b) are not sufficiently aware of what they do to teach it anyway!

The international student can be enormously aided in their task of understanding this new academic culture if the reasoning behind lectures, tutorials, seminars, essays, projects etc. can be explained.

For example, take those students who come from a culture where tutors occupy a strong authority role and direct all the studying and teaching. Consider how disconcerting it must be to a student to have to prepare an essay (possibly in their second or third language) in a situation where the tutor is not specific about what is required, other than a relevant response to the title, where the purpose of essays has not been explained, where the style and structure of writing essays has not been offered and so on.

This subject alone has many implications for the process of higher education. Culture will effect the extent to which participation and dialogue is achieved in seminars, indeed will effect all behaviours in the teaching situation. Often, however, it is not recognised that this behaviour is a result of cultural differences.

Consequently, it is often judged by the perceiver from their own cultural position, a judgement that invariably can be negative. (More can be read on this subject in Hall, E.T. (1954 & 1966), Hofstede, G. (1980) and Lago, C.O. (1990 & 1992).)

Other important factors about international students include:

a) They are not an homogeneous group. There are vast ranges of difference in culture and belief and personalities of any cohort of international students.

b) Students come from a variety of home backgrounds, some from very eminent families and positions in their own countries and others from rural communities funded by the state.

c) Purposes for attending certain courses can also be multifarious. Simple assumptions about motivation are worth avoiding.

d) The settling in period of the first year can be most difficult. International students consult Student Health Services much more during their first year of stay according to research.

e) Complexities of funding and visa requirements can also impose extra strains upon international students.

Useful contacts in relation to International students are:

● Debora Green, Department of Student Services ext 21266

● Jo Holliday, Student Advice Centre ext 28662

● United Kingdom Council for Overseas Student Affairs - 10171 226 3373

14. REFERRAL

For most students the University experience represents a major transition in life. For traditional undergraduate students (18 years old) this transition occurs with the period of growth labelled "late adolescence/early adulthood". Transition for international students will include the multiplicity of difficulties associated with culture shock. "Mature" students may have made major commitments to and demands on personal and familial links to attend University. The more vulnerable students may require a different or deeper level of support than the personal tutor, with the limits of his/her role, can provide. It is important to identify these students and arrange early referral.

REFERRAL GUIDELINES

1. Know the University and community resources for different kinds of services.

2. Explore clients readiness for referral. Have they expressed interest in specialist help? Are they afraid of seeing a counsellor, doctor or other helper? Do we frighten students with the implication of the severity of their problem?

3. Be direct and honest about your observation of the behaviour that led to your suggested referral. Be honest about your own limitations.

4. It is sometimes desirable to discuss the possibility of referral with the referral agency before the problem becomes urgent.

5. Determine which other persons have had contact with this client and confer with them before suggesting further steps, bearing in mind, however, the constraints of confidentiality.

6. Be fair in the explaining of services of a referral agency by citing the possi-bilities and the limitations of that agency. Do not imply that miracles can be performed there.

7. Do not release information to any referral source without permission from clients.

8. If you have the primary helping relationship with the client, it is only ethical to maintain the relationship until the referral is complete and as a new relationship is begun.

SOME THOUGHTS ON THE REFERRAL PROCESS

Wynn Bramley, in her book "Personal Tutoring in Higher Education" identified 13 different ways in which referrals were made to her Counselling Service by tutors.(1977) Some of these are definitely to be avoided if possible! Reading through them may help to clarify your thinking about why you would like to refer a student for counselling. Wynn Bramley refers to the phenomena of 'holding' which is a useful concept to have in mind in working with students. It refers to the process of keeping a student and his/her difficulties in your mind as you try to help them so that the student feels supported or "held" by you as opposed to feeling alone and overwhelmed by problems. 'Holding' takes place when a student is being seen by an effective helper but also when the student is absent but feels someone somewhere has his/her best interests in mind.

1. Symptom Referral

The tutor decides whether a referral is in order or not by the student's behaviour, but fails to uncover the meaning of such behaviour. An example of this would be where a student is affected by appropriate grief after a bereavement and cannot work normally for the period immediately following the loss. The tutor may respond by making a referral when in fact the student just needs time to adjust.

2. The Delayed Referral

This is when the tutor becomes more and more involved with a student, who meanwhile becomes emotionally dependent on the exhausted and often confused tutor. The counsellor is brought in too late, and the student finds it hard to transfer his or her trust and is angry at being 'ditched' by the tutor.

3. The Abandonment Referral

This is opposite to the delayed referral. A very early referral can be made, and the student then feels rejected. It is important, whenever a referral is made, that the student should be assured of the tutor's continued interest.

4. The Premature Referral

Students often need time and psychological 'holding' before they are ready to consider counselling. An interim period of thought and discussion is often needed before the student can feel happy about referral. Such a period of reflection and contemplation, within the context of a calm and trusting relationship with the tutor, often renders referral unnecessary.

5. The Unnecessary Referral

This often happens when tutors underestimate the capacity of students to help themselves or when they undervalue their own ability to help the students. It happens, too, when the student is in fact receiving and appreciating the support from the tutor, but the tutor feels guilty about not removing the student's pain quickly enough.

6. The Panic Referral

This too is often related to the tutor's inability to tolerate stress in the student and the mistaken feeling that a good tutor would find some painless and rapid way of alleviating the distress. Students in temporary trouble often behave in a dramatic and emotional way, which requires 'holding', and the tutor is panicked by the behaviour itself rather than the meaning of the behaviour.

7. The Rapid Referral

The student is very ill and in need of urgent medical attention and probably hospitalisation or physical restraint. It is too late for 'holding'. This is an emergency, and needs to be treated as such. The University Health Service or the student's G.P. in the city may need to be involved in this case.

8. Enforced Referral

This can occur when the student is quite content with the tutor, but the tutor feels more should be done, or when the tutor is more concerned about the student's condition than the student is. The tutor may have quite accurately recognised a relatively serious malady, but if the student is unwilling, coercion is rarely productive. Referral at a later date might be more fruitful when the problem has worsened and the student recognises the seriousness of the problem.

9. The 'Surgeon' Referral

The tutor and perhaps other staff and/or students find the student's behaviour or attitude offensive, disturbing, or embarrassing. There is a wish to 'cut away' unwanted aspects of the student's behaviour and little realisation that even if the student is willing, and even if change is possible via psychotherapeutic means, the rest of the personality is likely to be affected too. Magical expectations of the counsellor's or doctor's ability to whisk away symptoms inevitably lead to disappointment for both tutor and student.

10. The Ethical Referral

The tutor sensibly refers any student problems which s/he knows has a very strong attitudinal bias, which could reduce his/her objectivity if s/he were to handle the situation alone.

11.The Gradual Referral

The tutor refers in stages; at first talking with the student; then sharing feelings about the student and his/her own ability or inability to handle the case, with the counsellor, before deciding whether to refer the student formally. This is particularly important where there are fears that the student might feel abandoned if referred, or where there is already a warm and trusting relationship between student and tutor which could be jeopardized by a premature referral.

12.The Identification Referral

The tutor wisely recognises that the tutee's problem is very close to difficult areas in his or her own personality and referral might reduce the chances of becoming too entangled with the student's emotional life to the detriment of the tutor's own helping capacity.

13. The Non-Referral

A few tutors, whose urgent need to help is rooted in personality problems of their own, making them unduly possessive of students, are unable to refer them on when necessary. Unfortunately some fellow-students and even counsellors sometimes suffer from this unhelpful and rather desperate need to help.

Clearly many of these referral patterns are interwoven and cannot really be identified as separate entities. If in doubt, the suggestion of referral, made to a student in good faith, can do little harm. If the referral is rejected and the tutor is uncertain of how to proceed, an approach to the Counselling Service might be the next step.

VIGNETTES

INTRODUCTION

You may want to consider the following vignettes and how you would respond in such circumstances to a student in trouble. Also consider which resources or services you may wish to consult or refer the student to.

VIGNETTE i

Jeannette was 29 years old. She had left school at 16 with several 'O' levels to her name and had then worked as a secretary. She had realised over the years that she would always be bored in the jobs that she did and had studied at night school to gain good 'A' levels. She moved from a neighbouring town to a small flat located very near to the department in which she had registered. Although apparently a sociable and out-going young woman she had always had less confidence in herself than others realised and believed that she was extremely unattractive to the opposite sex. She was self-critical and deprecating about her abilities.

University was a great shock to Jeannette who felt bewildered and overawed by the large numbers of students in her department. She felt everyone was looking at her with the same critical thoughts that she had about herself. She had not made a single friend in her department. Since her flat was so close-by she would often skip lectures and retreat home. A pattern began to develop so that she avoided more and more lectures and would have panic attacks if she tried to force herself to go into the largest of the lecture theatres. She managed to speak to one lecturer once and told her she felt very threatened by the large numbers in the room. The lecturer took to placing her briefcase on a seat in the front row so that Jeannette could arrive at the last minute and still find a seat.

She also suggested that it would be helpful to explain the situation to her personal tutor so that she did not get behind in her work.

Jeannette found her tutor to be a pleasant, kindly man who was quick to reassure her that a student of her calibre need not be unduly worried about keeping up with the work. He suggested that if she read the books on the reading list she would be able to catch up with missed work. He agreed to send her the booklist and to get notes from other students.

By the end of the first year Jeannette had still been unable to procure the booklist and was missing most lectures and seminars. The personal tutor was on leave. The panic attacks increased with the approach of first year exams which she failed.Jeanette was left feeling very angry with the university and with herself.

There are several ways in which Jeannette could have helped herself but also some different strategies that the department could have adopted. You might like to pause and reflect awhile before considering just a few of the options below.

Some strategies to consider:

1. Some informal but structured exercises could have helped students get to know each other or at least to break the ice in seminars and lectures at the beginning of the year.

2. Personal tutors can arrange informal meetings with their tutorial group as a whole in the first few weeks of term and contact anyone who appears to be isolating themselves.

3. Listen carefully to what a student is telling you. Reassurance is not always reassuring. Make sure students know if you are going to be absent for a long time and don't promise anything you can't deliver (however, we all make mistakes and forget things!).

4. If a student is having panic attacks or seems to be displaying notable features of anxiety suggest that they think about referring themselves to the Counselling Service or to the Health Service. While panic attacks are very common they do need to be taken seriously, especially if they are linked to substantial avoidance behaviour.

5. Make sure the student knows that an organisation exists for them (MSA) and that there also exists a Mature Student Adviser whom they can contact.

6. Keep an eye out for students who disappear at the drop of a hat and try to create opportunities for conversation even if this is only a matter of exchanging pleasantries. Departments can seem very unwelcoming to students who are not at ease with themselves.

VIGNETTE ii

Mark was a 3rd year student who seemed to be both satisfactory in academic terms and well adjusted to student life. He was involved with various sporting activities, enjoyed good friendships and had managed to secure a job on graduation.

Three weeks before his final exams Mark appeared at his tutor's door in an anxious state. He had been in a fight with some local lads a month previously after being provoked for no immediately apparent reason. He did not usually fight but on this occasion he had felt very justified and lashed out. The fracas was brief and Mark walked off with the friends back to hall. He had then avoided that part of town. Last night however, he had been invited by some different friends to meet in a pub near where the incident had taken place. He was waiting to meet his friends when he was spotted by one of the people with whom he had fought. The young man called the police who arrested Mark on a very serious charge. He was to appear in court in the next 2 weeks. He was convinced he would go to prison and that he would not be able to sit his finals.

Again, you may like to reflect on what you would do in this situation. Below are a few suggestions, but by no means are they the only ones.

Some thoughts to consider:

1. How much does Mark's anxiety reflect an accurate picture of what is likely to happen? Does he need time to talk and think about what he should do? If so can you give him time now, if not, when?

2. Does he lack sufficient information to understand the likely outcomes of a court case? If this is so you may want to put him in contact with an advisor in the Students' Union Advisory Service. The Students' Union will also be able to supply him with the name of a lawyer who has worked with other students in the past.

3. Are you able to give him an idea about whether or not he will be able to postpone his court-case or postpone his exams? If not, can you let him know when you can give him the information? Who might you need to contact?

4. Is there more to this story than meets the eye? Is Mark getting so anxious he needs more professional help? If so you may need to consider a referral to counselling.

15. HELPING STUDENTS LEARN

STUDY SKILLS

Whilst study skills belong really to the remit of the academic tutor it is sometimes useful to bear in mind that our very earliest experiences of learning occurred when we were small children within the context of the child-parent relationship. When academic work goes badly wrong the student may be overwhelmed by feelings that seem to have little relation to the rather concrete, perhaps even mundane tasks in hand. Learning and studying are not simply intellectual activities but involve emotional experience. Most tutors will have already encountered the painful situation where a student seems unable to make academic decisions, cannot limit or focus work or complete projects. The student may become agitated and even troublesome, not unlike an insecure child who clings to the tutor and wants to be told exactly what to write. In this kind of situation there is a place for gentle reassurance, calm repetition of what needs to be done and firmness. It may help to keep in mind the image of a good parent who can contain the child's anxiety without overreacting by becoming angry or overprotective. Such students often find their way to counselling and if in agreement may well benefit from a collaborative approach between tutor and counsellor.

At other times, especially the beginning of the academic year, new students may feel so disorientated that they really do not take in all clear instructions given to them. Again their anxiety is such that they fail to perform the simplest of tasks effectively (like finding their way to the correct lecture theatre).

It would be too much to present here an exposition of learning and studying difficulties and their relation to emotional states but there are some books which tutors may find interesting if they would like to follow up this area. The library has an excellent selection of books on study skills and the Counselling Service also has a small collection of books. If departments can organize study skills workshops geared specifically to their own subjects then students are even better served, but if this is not possible the following books may be useful:-

Acres, D.   *How to Pass Exams Without Anxiety*
                 How to Books, Plymouth.

Buzan, T.   *Speed Reading! Great Britain*
                 Sphere Books Ltd 1971

Buzan, T.   *Use Your Head*
                 London, BBC 1974

Northedge, A.   *The Good Study Guide*
                 Open University 1990

Osborne, E.   *The Emotional Experience of Learning and Teaching*
Saltzberge-   Routledge Education Books. London 1987
Witterberg
& Henry, G.

EXAMS: "STORM AND STRESS"

There are three aspects of anxiety related to exams which need to be thought about separately. Firstly students may have trouble preparing themselves realistically in terms of revision technique. This is often a cause of apprehension in students who have not recently taken 'A' levels. Secondly, students may be well equipped to prepare themselves but be less able to perform to their own satisfaction in the given amount of time allowed in the exam situation. Finally, going completely to pieces in the exam itself and fear of this phenomenon is yet another issue. Help with structuring revision timetables and guidelines on appropriate areas of revision are evidently important to discuss. Sometimes exam technique itself needs some attention with opportunities for timed essays or attempts to make notes on past papers. These sorts of things are grist to the mill of most academics who may be willing to tackle these areas with individuals or groups. The Counselling Service also organises occasional workshops on coping with exams. The successful overcoming of exam panic or the anticipation of such panic requires a more psychological approach.

In his paper 'Examination Anxiety: What the Student Counsellor Can Do' Windy Dryden found that students who knew they would have difficulty with 'nerves' did well if they commenced a course of relaxation training some time before they were due to sit exams. The relaxation helped not only with staying in control in the exam situation but also improved revision and recall in the period before the exam. There are several ways in which students can find opportunities to learn relaxation techniques. They can join a regular but informal relaxation group run by the Counselling Service. Alternatively they can enrol on Yoga courses in the University and elsewhere or buy relaxation tapes commercially or from the Counselling Service. Tutors can play a helpful role in encouraging the student to start such training well in advance of exams. If there is a need, a referral can be made to the Counselling Service for more individual help. The Student Health Service is also able to prescribe appropriate medication if self-help techniques founder or there is not time to spare and are also able to allow students to sit exams in the Ranmoor Clinic in situations of severe distress or illness if the student and tutor are able to make the necessary arrangements.

Useful books and tapes:

Acres, D.   *How to Pass Exams Without Anxiety*
              How to Books, Plymouth 1987

Dryden, W.   *Examination Anxiety: what the Student*
              Counsellor Can Do
              British Journal of Guidance & Counselling
              Vol. 6, No. 3

Gibb, G.   *Teaching Students to Learn*
              A Student-Centred Approach
              Milton Keynes Open University Press 1981

16. WORKING WITH GROUPS

"In the Eastern martial art of aikido the warrior learns, 'never to go against the opponent's strength', but rather to blend with and redirect the energy of his/her attacker. The aikido master knows how to, 'touch softly and gently' in order to use the power already generated by the adversary. In the midst of motion and conflict there is an exact point to apply pressure and a precise intervention that will subdue the attack. In contrast to this 'way of gentle harmony', the Western disciplines of boxing and wrestling are characterized by collision and force over-whelming force.

The aikido master is a metaphor for the effective group worker who rather than fight or wrestle knows how to be in harmony with the group. He or she can utilize the pressure points and redirect and employ collective energy and power to take the simplest path towards the desired goal. The simplest path is revealed by awareness and understanding of the meaning of individual and group needs, behaviour, and interaction. Unless he or she is attentive to and knowledgeable about what is happening inside the system in which they operate an effective group worker cannot adequately determine what is the most appropriate way to intervene or respond."

Reference unknown.

INTRODUCTION

Much of the emphasis of this booklet has been upon the skills required of working well with individuals. Not surprisingly, different complex dynamics occur when working with groups of people. Nevertheless, some of the skills of communication dealt with earlier will apply, e.g.

- Appropriate attention - giving

- Listening skills

- Seeking Understanding/clarifying

- Respecting the other person and their views

- Being clear about how much time is available

- Uninterrupted time

Also, the contents of Appendix One, entitled "Creating the Conditions for Learning" will provide a guide to the importance of setting a climate for group work.

In continuing the theme of climate setting, Dr George Brown of Nottingham University makes the following points

> "The key word in my approach to small groups is safety. The tutor must make it possible for everybody to feel safe in the group. Safe to contribute; safe to try out new ideas; safe to relax.

> Safety is vital because so many seminars are ruled by fear. The student fears that the tutor or the other students will make him or her look stupid. The tutor fears that his or her own ignorance may be exposed or that they may lose control of the group. This kills the seminar."

The positive group that is supportive of the members as people has a minimum display of personal attacking and judging/ evaluating behaviours.

Part of the climate setting function of the leader then, is to create an ambience of safety and participation and some of this can be achieved through the way the group is started. Introductions all round, invitations to participate, sharing or negotiating a contract with the participants which might include points about the time-keeping, smoking or not, the nature of confidentiality (or not), the intentions of the group etc. Further, it can be useful, where applicable, to negotiate an agenda with the group, thus attempting to ensure that the variety of needs or expectations in the group are recorded an can be addressed later.

Often in groups, our focus as leaders or tutors, is on the content of the discussion, the theme that is being discussed. A successful group leader also takes note of the interpersonal processes, the dynamics between the participants themselves.

The learning which takes place in groups may be categorised as:

Cognitive   Knowledge of facts, ideas and skills. Logical analysis, clear thinking, evaluating ideas, problem solving, perceiving new relationships and imaginative thinking can all be developed in small groups.

Social Affective   Social insight, self-awareness, awareness of others, understanding of others and negotiation skills can all be developed in small groups.

This distinction between these categories of cognitive learning and social-affective learning is arbitrary.

Often they merge into one another yet both categories are important. There is unlikely to be cognitive learning unless the social-affective basis of the group is sound.

There is unlikely to be social learning unless the group used their cognitive skills.

Most tutors are concerned primarily with cognitive tasks. Nonetheless attention to the social-affective life of a group is absolutely necessary if the group is going to work efficiently and effectively.

Unlike lecturing, the tutor's task within groups becomes multifaceted. Tutors need to be able to:-

a) provide information when required

b) stimulate debate to enable students to discuss the subject

c) encourage participation amongst quieter members

d) listen well

e) question skilfully (so as to stimulate further thought and at the same time not create threat or fear)

f) communicate their understanding of individuals

g) summarise, from time to time, the main views or points made.

h) manage their own opinions satisfactorily, (thus recognising the difference between factual data and their own interpretations of that data) thus offering the group clarity when they contribute themselves.

LEVELS OF PARTICIPATION

The level of participation by individuals in groups is influenced by a considerable range of factors, e.g.

A. *Personal Concerns*

What else is happening, at a personal level, in a certain person's life at the time. As a group leader you may never be informed or come to know anything about this intrapersonal world of any or some of the group members. If they are pre-occupied with personal concerns, or have previously experienced groups as threatening or are tired out... there are many such personal reasons. Try, therefore, not to jump to simple conclusions or judgements about anyone's apparently non co-operative behaviour. Appropriate caution should be exercised in exploring this personal dimension with the person concerned, especially in a group setting.

B. *The Topic*

In general the less interested an individual is in the topic, the less s/he will contribute. The occasional individual will rebel and participate highly putting forward objections or trying to change what the group is doing.

C. *Group Climate*

A positive group i.e. one that is supportive of the members as people and has a minimum of personal attacking and judging (evaluating), will encourage the participation of all the group members.

D. *Self-Esteem*

An individual with high esteem is less dependent on the approval of others and hence will be less influenced by a negative, hostile, evaluative group climate. Such an individual will tend to participate more than someone with a low opinion of her or himself.

E. Communication Skills

Individuals already skilled in communicating - putting their thoughts into words will be more ready to do so than individuals whose skills are low. Where it is the case that some individuals are low in skills then strategies which enable them to improve their skills will be needed.

F. Group Size

This affects the participation as the larger the group the less time is available per person. This will tend to intensify the difficulties of those who find it hard to participate, whatever the cause.

G. Group Composition

Having group members with a wide range of esteem or skills will result in very uneven participation. As a group continues to meet, people who are low participators (for whatever reason) tend to become less involved and committed even where original involvement was high.

ALTERNATIVE WAYS FOR WORKING WITH GROUPS

Sometimes the level of participation in group work can be changed and enhanced by offering alternative structures for the group to work within. A list is given below of a variety of these approaches.

Lecturing   A lecture to a small group.

Controlled Discussion   Strict control by tutor.

Step-by-Step Discussion Planned sequence of issues/questions.

Seminar   Group discussion of a paper.

Case Discussion   Presentation of case then attempts at solution.

Problem Centred   Similar to above, but often more quantitative.

Problems Class   Individuals working on problems or presenting solutions.

Tutorial	Meeting with very small group, often based on essay.
Group Tutorial	Topic and direction from tutor, rest from group.
Free Discussion	Topic and direction from group, tutor observes.
Tutorless Group	Some direction from tutor, group may report back.
Self-Help Group	Run by and for students, tutor may be a resource.
Cross-Over Groups	Brief discussions then transfers between groups.
Buzz Group	Very brief discussions generating ideas for following up.
Snowballing	Pairs becoming small groups becoming larger groups.
Syndicate	Mini-project work reported to full class.
Brain-Storming	Brief generation of ideas. No criticism. Quantity.
Simulation / Game	Structured experience in real/imaginary roles.
Role-Play	Less structured activity in allocated or self-created roles.
Fishbowl	Small groups within large then discussion and reversal.
Workshop	Mixture of methods usually directed at attitudes and skills.
Demonstrations	Illustrations of theoretical principles.
Exercises	Tightly structured experiments or provide data.
Structured Enquiries	Lightly structured experiments, more student input.
Open-Ended Enquiries	Students determine structure and report back.
Projects	Student research. tutor provides supervision.

Personalised System of Instruction (PSI)	Self paced. Tests on progress.
Computer Assisted Learning (CAL)	Often to simulate experiments etc.
Learning Aids Laboratory	Miniature resource centre AV material.

Of necessity, this section is relatively short, given the complex nature of group work. Several books are listed blow which deal with the subject in much more detail. Also, colleagues interested in developing their skills in this area are encouraged to attend training courses where both the cognitive and experiential elements of the subject are explored. Courses within the University are occasionally run by the Staff Development Unit. Outside organisations like the Tavistock Institute for Human Relations in London also run a wide spectrum of training courses.

BIBLIOGRAPHY

Abercrombie, M.L.J.   *Aims and Techniques of Group Teaching*
                          S.R.H.E. publication (1970)

Jacques, D.(1984)   *Learning in Groups*
                          Croom Helm

Lewis, H.R.(1979)   *The Anatomy of Small Groups*
                          Studies in Higher Education
                          Vol. 4, No. 2, p.269

17. TUTORS REFLECTIONS ON THE TUTORING ROLE

A THE JOYS, SORROWS AND CHALLENGES OF BEING A PERSONAL TUTOR

"Am I interrupting you?"

"No, I was just waiting for something to happen".

There seem to be three reasons why personal tutees arrive. They come because they have been "sent for", because they need "support and advice" and to "rejoice".

SENT FOR

Personal tutees who come because they are expected to see their personal tutor are an experience of banging my head against a wall. They see me so infrequently that it is difficult for us to have a really relaxed relationship. When I ask how they are the answer is often "alright" or "O.K." and (unspoken) "I don't intend to share my life/problems with a stranger". Trying to read between the lines raises the problem of legitimacy for me - is it legitimate for me to doubt their "O.K.", to say "You don't sound very sure that you are O.K.". I do probe a bit, but I always feel uncomfortable, and I'm rarely let into their world.

SUPPORT AND ADVICE

Tutees asking for advice I find difficult. I slip into "If I was you.." with the ease of a natural. But I am not them. I am not a troubled nineteen year old; and I haven't been for thirty years; and my memories of that age fade; and the world has changed! So I try and stay out of advice giving - it usually is a waste of time.

Those needing support are a main purpose of personal tutors. I can "open doors" for them, jump them up queues, bend regulations, and I have two ears and a big box of paper hankies. Often they just need to share with someone who isn't a threat.

After 25 years of personal tutoring I have at last found that it helps to say (instead of just observing) "You look sad/upset/frightened/confused/angry etc. etc." "You look sad". often releases the tears they have been unhelpfully struggling to control: But if you are frightened of tears, sadness etc., etc. then the line "You look sad..." is not for you as a tutor.

REJOICE

When personal tutees come to rejoice it is a rich reward for the time you have given them - the exam success, the crisis overcome or averted, the job secured.

Hurray!

Duncan Kitchin
B.Sc. (Econ) M.Sc. (O.D.)
Lecturer in Management Studies

B SOME REFLECTIONS ON PERSONAL TUTORING

One of the fascinating aspects of tutorial work with students is its varied nature. No two individuals are identical and though problems may appear similar they are never exactly the same.

From a tutor's point of view some of the most disappointing cases are those individuals who have no interest in their work, no motivation and simply regard their stay at university as an opportunity to have a good time. Fortunately there are usually only a few such errant characters, but it takes up a disproportionate amount of time chasing them up and this time is largely wasted. It is often a mystery why they came to the university at all.

Perhaps the saddest cases are those whose problems are very real and appear to have no acceptable solution. The most common problem, which I have come across, is that of women students caught between different cultures. They are usually people who have been born in this country, educated in British schools and yet come from an ethnic background where parents chose a suitable husband for them etc. Such women have aspirations of their own and want to decide their own future but they often love their parents and are loath to make a break with them which is the only way in which they can hope to gain their independence. As in so many cases the only course of action is to provide as much help and support as possible and sometimes the future takes a totally unexpected turn which provides an easing, or even a solution, of the situation.

One of the great joys of being a tutor is the sense of achievement which arises on the occasions when help and support is seen to have been of value. The evidence may take the form of examination success for individuals who have struggled in lectures and have required extra help in order to be able to understand their academic work or for those with weighty personal or family problems who have needed support until their difficulties were alleviated.

Friendships, thus forged, often survive long after the final examinations. It is always a great joy to hear from former students over the years.

I would like to think that we can continue to give students the same individual care and attention in the future as we have done in the past. Sadly, however, this is probably totally unrealistic given the rising student numbers.

Mary Hart
Tutor in the Department of Pure Mathematics

C SOME DIFFERENT APPROACHES TO SUPPORTING STUDENTS

1. We introduced a system of tutors for MSc students a few years ago. This was at the request of the staff-student committee. Each MSc. student is allocated a member of staff as their tutor. We then leave it up to the students to approach their tutor when necessary.

   At first sight it might seem that this would increase our work load substantially. This has not been our experience, however. What the system represents is a support mechanism that is available when required. I think that this provides a useful point of reference if a problem arises that cannot be solved elsewhere. Very few students actually make use of it but knowing that it's there is the important thing. Also there is a specific secretary who deals with MSc students and she is a vital component in our pastoral care mechanism.

2. These MSc students also do a major group project during 2 terms which is managed by experienced project managers we hire from industry. They provide a fairly tight structure and control mechanism that prevents students from becoming disorientated or depressed about trying to progress a large and difficult project. This also helps in maintaining morale and momentum.

3. In our undergraduate programme each 1st year student is allocated to a tutor along with 3 - 4 other students. They meet as a group with their tutor every week and embark on a group project that lasts for one and a half terms. They learn about groupworking, about gathering, analysing and presenting information in this context. The tutor is able to provide expertise, support and guidance in what is often a very new and potentially stressful activity.

Professor Mike Holcombe
Department of Computer Science

18. RESOURCES AND SERVICES IN THE UNIVERSITY AND THE STUDENTS' UNION

A comprehensive guide of the services provided by the University and the Students' Union is published annually and is available from the Central Student Services, Firth Court.

Space has been left below to insert details of the appropriate departments and personnel pertinent to your needs.

APPENDIX I

CREATING THE CONDITIONS FOR LEARNING

More than twenty years ago, after much experience and observation, the eminent American psychologist and educator, Carl Rogers, came to the conclusion that personality change in individual psychotherapy was made possible primarily by certain attitudinal qualities in the therapist. These essential attitudes were, he hypothesized, three in number. First was what he termed congruence. This meant what was being experienced by the therapist was evident in his words and behaviour. He was somehow 'transparent' in the relationship. There was no facade, no pretence. He or she was a real person in the relationship. The second attitude was a prizing of the client, an unconditional, non-judgemental caring. The third attitude was an empathic quality, an ability to understand the inner world of the client, as the client perceived it, and an ability to express this understanding. The therapist's empathy was seen as one of the most powerful elements in facilitating change.

Over the years, research in the field of counselling and psychotherapy has on the whole borne out the significance of these attitudes. They appear to be more significant than the length of therapist training, the particular school of thought of the therapist, more important than the therapist's diagnostic skill. The significance of these three qualities have been extensively validated in psychotherapy.

For many years, however, no in-depth study of these attitudes had been made in education.

Here is where a giant amongst educational researchers, David Aspy, comes in. He had decided upon a major study to determine what teacher behaviours were correlated with various kinds of learning outcomes. He developed a long list of teacher behaviours, and among them he included the attitudes Rogers had found important in therapy, slightly redefined to fit the educational situation. Of all the variable studies, these turned out to be the most significant - the teacher's realness, respect for the student and understanding of the meaning of the classroom experience to the student.

Very briefly, the method that Aspy and his colleague, Roebuck, employed was first to obtain tape-recorded hours of classroom instruction. Rating scales were developed to assess various degrees of these three ordinary attitudes and behaviours, ranging from low to high.

Using these three scales, unbiased raters measured the 'facilitative conditions' as exhibited by each teacher. These ratings were then correlated with achievement test scores, with problem solving ability, with number of absences from class - the range of variable was very great.

Having established a methodology, the researchers applied it on a previously unheard of scale. Their final report indicates that they recorded and assessed nearly 3,700 hours of classroom instruction, from 550 elementary and secondary school teachers! These studies were done in various parts of the United States and in several other countries, including Great Britain. They involved black, white and Mexican American teachers and students. No study of comparable magnitude had even been made.

Here is the summary of the findings of Aspy and his colleagues:

1. There was a clear correlation between the facilitative conditions provided by the teacher and academic achievement of students. This finding has been repeatedly confirmed. Students of 'high level' teachers (those high in the facilitative conditions) tended to show the greatest gains in learning. A sobering finding was that students of 'low-level' teachers may actually be retarded in their learning by deficiency.

2. The situation most conducive to learning was when teachers who exhibited high levels of the conditions were backed up and supervised by head teachers with similarly high levels. Under these conditions, students not only showed greater gains in school subjects but other positive gains as well. They became more adept at using their higher cognitive processes such as problem-solving. (This was especially noteworthy where the teacher showed a high degree of positive regard and respect. Creative problem-solving evidently requires a nurturant climate).

- They had a more positive self concept than was found in other groups.

- They initiated more behaviour in the class room.

- They exhibited fewer discipline problems.

- They had a lower rate of absence from school.

In one exciting study, they even showed an increase in IQ. In this study, 25 black first graders with 'high level' teachers and 25 with 'low level' teachers, were given individual intelligence tests nine months apart. The first group showed an average IQ increase from 85 to 94. The figures for the second group were 84 and 84 - no change whatsoever.

3. Teachers can improve in the level of facilitative conditions with as little as 15 hours of carefully planned intensive training, involving both cognitive and experiential learning. Considering the demonstrated influence of these attitudinal conditions it is highly important to know that they can be increased.

4. Of significance for all of education is the finding that teachers improve in these attitudes only when their trainers exhibit a high level of these facilitative conditions. In ordinary terms, this means that such attitudes are 'caught' experientially from another. They are not simply intellectual learnings.

5. Teachers exhibiting high levels of facilitative conditions tend to have other characteristics:

- They have a more positive self-concept than low level teachers.

- They are more self-disclosing to their students

- They respond more to students feelings.

- They give more praise.

- They lecture less often.

6. Neither geographical location of the classes, racial composition, or race of the teacher altered these findings.

Aspy and Roebuck summarised all these studies in one sentence: "It pays to be **human** in the classroom!" Whether at the elementary or secondary school level, it seemed clear that the most important things the teacher could do was to provide a facilitative learning climate. Such a classroom atmosphere would be marked by the teacher's realness, caring and understanding listening. Under such conditions his or her other behaviours were less important. It was also evident that in such a climate students developed their own motivation for learning.

Carl Rogers himself, reflecting on this study, could see only one possible flaw. It seemed too good to be true. Could it really be possible that the very same relationship conditions which fostered self-learning and self-insight in psychotherapy would also foster the learning of mathematics or a foreign language? He could find no defect in the research design and statistics, and he wanted to believe the findings were correct but he somehow had an inner reservation.

Shortly afterwards, on a separate research programme, Dr Reinhardt Tausch in Germany replicated the findings of Aspy and Roebuck.

There are some who may wish to argue that all this elaborate research might be of interest to school teachers but has little to say to university lecturers who are, after all, concerned with knowledge of a much more advanced variety and the cultivation of critical faculties with 'rapier-like potential'. Yet, if such facilitative attitudes are critical in the counselling relationship, it seems to me that we would be very arrogant indeed to ignore the immense importance of this work and its possible application in the sectors of further and higher education".

Extracts from First Annual Counselling Lecture at Sheffield University, given by Brian Thorne, The Director of Counselling at the University of East Anglia.

Most of the material is drawn directly from an unpublished paper by Carl Rogers entitled *Education - a Personal Activity*, 1980.

Extensive reference to Aspy and Roebuck's work may be found in Rogers, C.R.R., *Freedom to Learn for the '80s*, Merrill, London, (pp. 221 -223), 1983

APPENDIX II

A SAMPLE JOB DESCRIPTION FOR TUTORS

This job description is designed as a stimulus for discussion and not as a model to be adopted unthinkingly. It represents an attempt to pull together the various ideas and processes identified in the manual in a form which will help tutors to clarify their areas of responsibility and involvement.

1. General

i) The aims of the tutorial role in vocational preparation are to encourage students to take increasing responsibility for their own learning and development, and to help students overcome any blocks to such a process.

ii) Tutors are encouraged to get to know the students for whom they have a tutorial responsibility in order to help them take decisions and choices based on knowledge and thought rather than on ignorance and chance.

iii) Tutors are expected to pay particular attention to the expressed needs of their students at the stages of selection, induction, academic experience (including assessment), and transition.

2. Specific

Tutors are expected to take part in the following tasks with individual students and/or with groups.

i) Having due regard to the inevitable constraints, to take part in discussion with the student, employers, careers staff and others involved, in order to determine the opportunity available which is most appropriate to the student.

ii) To discuss with the student his/her expectations of the college, the course, and the individual tutor, and the expectations they hold of him/her, to agree realistic offers and demands for one to take to/of the other.

iii) To ensure that other teaching staff and/or, where appropriate, others outside the college, understand their place in the provision of the student's learning programme.

iv) To provide the student with information and advice regarding the opportunity and regarding subsequent opportunities where relevant.

v) To check out periodically that the original contract is being adhered to by all the participants - students, tutors, supervisors etc.

vi) To explore the feelings and thoughts that lie behind the student's experience of difficulty or distress, or his/her hopes and fears for the future.

vii) To refer the student to the most appropriate person who can offer help.

viii) To review and record the student's progress and achievements through use of a variety of measures, including profiles.

ix) To offer teaching particularly in areas where the student lacks confidence (for example, in study skills).

x) To offer coaching for students who are having difficulty in certain aspects of their work.

xi) To confront students with the consequences of stepping over the limits set by the rules   and regulations of the college or other organisation (such consequences may include the application of sanctions).

xii) To speak for or act 'on behalf of' a student, perhaps at a disciplinary hearing.

xiii) To inform colleagues and management about issues affecting students that require course or organisational change to resolve.

xiv) To take part in investigating the effectiveness of the course for the student in relation to the agreed contract and stated aims.

(xv) To write references o provide other reports on student where appropriate.

Such a list of tasks is daunting, and it is not expected that each tutor will take on such a range of tasks for each student. The intention is rather that each task is available to each student. This means that a particularly important task for course teams is to determine 'who does what and by when?'

BIBLIOGRAPHY

Abercrombie, M.L.J., (1970)
Aims and Techniques of Group Teaching
S.R.H.E. Publications.

Acres, D. (1992)
How to Pass Exams Without Anxiety
Plymouth, How to Books

Adler, P.S. (1975)
The Transitional Experience: An Alternative View of Culture Shock
Journal of Humanistic Psychology.

Althen, G. (1997)
NAFSA Newsletter
February .

Aspy, D & Roebuck, F. (1983)
Extensive references to their work may be found in Rogers, C.R.R.
Freedom to Learn for the '80's
London. Merrill,

Bramley, W. (1977)
Personal Tutoring in Higher Education. Guildford: Society for Research in Higher Education.

Buzan, T. (1971)
Speed Reading!
phere Books.

Buzan, T. (1974)
Use Your Head
London, B.B.C.

Cooper, R. & N.
Culture Shock Thailand & How to Survive It.

Coffey, M. & Grace, S. (1997a)
Managing Anger and Saying No
International Educator. Summer Vol.VI, No.4, 31-34

Coffey, M. & Grace, S. (1997b)
Intercultural Advising in English language Programmes
Washington, D.C. NAFSA

Dryden, W. (1978)
Examination Anxiety: What the Student Counsellor Can Do.
British Journal of Guidance and Counselling. Vol.6. No.3. July

Fisher, S. (1989)
Homesickness, Cognition and Health
London. Lawrence Erlbaum Associates

Gibb, G. (1981)
Teaching Students to Learn - A Student-Centred Approach
Milton Keynes. Open University

Golan, N. (1981)
Passing Through Transitions: A guide for Practitioners
Free Press, U.S.A.

Gordon, T. (1980)
Leader Effectiveness Training
Bantam Books

Hall, E.T., (1954)
The Silent Language
New York. Doubleday

Hall, E.T. (1966)
The Hidden Dimension
New York. Doubleday

Heyno, A. (undated)
Dealing with Difficult and Disruptive Situations
University of Westminster

Hofstede, G. (1980)
Culture's Consequences: International Differences in Work - Related Values
Beverley Hills. Sage Publications

Jacques, D. (1984)
Learning in Groups
Croom Helm

Lago, C.O. (1990)
Working with Overseas Students: A Staff Development Manual
Huddersfield University and British Council

Lago, C.O. & Shipton, G.S. (1994)
On Listening and Learning:
Student Counselling in Further and Higher Education
London. Central Book Publishing

Lago, C.O. (1996)
Computer Therapeutics:
A New Challenge for Counsellors and Psychotherapists".
Counselling: The Journal of the British Association for Counselling. Rugby.
November. Vol.17. No.4

Lewis, H.R. (1979)
The Anatomy of Small Groups
Studies in Higher Education Vo.4. No.2.p269

Mathers, E. (undated)
What to do when a student seems mentally disturbed
University of Humberside

Miller, J.C. Tutoring: (1983)
The Guidance and Counselling Role in Vocational Preparation
National Institute for Careers Education and Counselling. February

Northedge, A. (1990)
The Good Study Guide. Milton Keynes

Osborne, E., Saltzberger Wittenberg & Henry, G. (1987)
The Emotional Experience of Learning and Teaching.
Routledge Education Books.

Rickenson, B. & Rutherford, D. (1995)
Increasing Student Retention.
British Journal of Guidance and Counselling.

Rickenson, B. (1996)
*Systematic Monitoring of the Adjustment to University of Undergraduates:
A Strategy for Reducing Withdrawal Rates.*
British Journal for Guidance and Counselling.

Tinto., V. (1975)
Dropout from Higher Education: A Theoretical Synthesis of Recent Research.
Review of Education Research. 45, pp.89-125.

Valentine, C.A. (1968)
Culture and Poverty
University of Chicago Press.